That
New-
time
Religion

That New-time Religion

THE JESUS REVIVAL IN AMERICA

ERLING JORSTAD

Best wishes & love always,

Erling

AUGSBURG PUBLISHING HOUSE
Minneapolis, Minnesota

THAT NEW-TIME RELIGION

MANUFACTURED IN THE UNITED STATES OF AMERICA

To Eric and Laura
"All things made new"

Contents

Introduction

A professor of evangelism, Robert E. Coleman, asks: "Will the world undergo a great revival before the end of the age? This possibility is increasingly discussed among Christians who believe that the last conclusive struggles of our civilization have begun." [1]

Billy Graham states: "But *something is happening.* There is a stirring in the mulberry bushes! The winds of renewal and revival are stirring! God is on the move. I am convinced that the harvest is the ripest it has ever been in American history. I do not believe it will ever be so ripe again. This is God's hour in America. Let's strike while the iron is hot." [2]

Among the signs of change which encouraged Graham was that of the large number of young people who were searching and questioning "as no other generation in American history, and thousands are turning to Christ."

One of the leading spokesmen for this youth movement, Duane Pederson, writes that its influence "is reaching a much wider group than just the street people. It is reaching into the Establishment Churches. . . . It is reaching across any and all denominational lines. . . . It is reaching across America. . . . In fact, it is reaching far beyond the boundaries of our land. This movement of the Holy Spirit is spreading like wildfire. And I believe it is the beginning of the most powerful revival in the history of the world. I don't like to think in terms of setting dates. But I do know that Jesus Christ will not be long in coming. This Movement—this generation—is just paving the way for him." [3]

Whether this new-time religion appears within Roman Catholic groups who are speaking in tongues, or among young adults moving to rural communes named "Living Waters" or "Love Inn," or at mass baptisms of teenagers along the Pacific coast, or among teeny boppers marching with "Turn On With Jesus" placards, the participants know they are being renewed and guided by the power of the Holy Spirit . And they are ready to follow wherever that leads.

The New Revival and the Churches

Like the earlier great revivals in American history, the current movement comes when the traditional denominations find themselves in decline on several fronts. For the first time since World War II, attendance at Sunday worship is appreciably down. A Gallup Poll in 1971

10

showed that 75 percent of all Americans believe that religion is losing its influence in American life—a figure five times higher than in 1957. Enrollment in parochial schools and some church related colleges has dropped noticeably, as has college enrollment in theology and church history courses. A drastic decline in financial resources among most of the largest church bodies has forced sharp cutbacks in programs. Many clergymen are indicating serious doubts about continuing in the ministry. And the most noticeable decline in church membership is among those under thirty.

This pattern of simultaneous renewal and decline suggests that revival is breaking out most strongly outside the organized denominations—Protestant and Catholic. Some observers call this movement "the underground church"; others consider it a "parachurch movement." Whatever the label, it is clear that tension among American Christians over the new-time religion is growing rapidly. Duane Pederson of the Jesus People recognizes this but insists that his followers are not anti-church. "It's just that we haven't been welcomed into too many churches; in fact we've been asked to leave churches." [4]

Thus for the first time in American church life a vigorous, national revival is breaking out and growing with little or no direct relationship to the churches. Contrary to earlier revivals, which generally helped strengthen the denominations, the new revival is drawing off energy, support, and prayers from the churches in need of such help.

Beyond that, today's new-time religion breaks sharply with older revivals because of its radically different attitude toward certain basic American institutions. Earlier revivalists made little or no public criticism of traditional American social institutions. Today's revival, however is characterized in large part by opposition or indifference to such institutions as the nuclear family, free enterprise, the work ethic, and the democratic processes of government. By its decision to work outside the established churches and to question some basic American social institutions, this revival stands as a *new-time religion.*

If this movement centered only on the teen-age Jesus People, or only on the Pentecostals, or only on the college evangelicals, it might not be so serious a challenge to the churches. But because it embraces so many different activities and age groups, it constitutes a new kind of problem for the churches—who are having enough problems without this one. The possibility of recovery and new life for the old-time churches may be determined by the success they have in reconciling the new-time religion with their traditional teachings and practices.

This call to reform is not simply a matter of surface change. One can worship with a guitar as well as a pipe organ; one can experience a sense of community in an urban coffee house as well as in the traditional Fellowship Hall of the local church. The far more challenging task will be to find areas of reconciliation in some of the historically divisive teachings of the new revivalism: millennial eschatology; instant conversion and total immersion; a personal rather than social outreach to the disadvantaged in society; speaking in tongues; a minimal interest in the scholarly study of the Bible, theology, and church history; and a total unconcern for polity. As will be shown below, all these have tended to divide American churches far more than they have united them. This possibility is again facing us.

And if these issues are not divisive enough, more political ones will surely keep the controversy alive for the foreseeable future—issues such as pacifism, nonviolent resistance, suspicion of capitalism, and glorification of communal living and sharing of property. All these are a part of the new-time religion.

Controversy Over Revival

Revivals have always attracted public attention, and today's is no exception. Those who believe in revival see it as a tremendous outpouring of the power of the Holy Spirit sweeping across the land. They see it as direct answer to prayer, and they respond with joy, enthusiasm, and gratitude for this visible sign of God's continuing presence.

At times in America's past such enthusiasm has led believers to show their joy in unconventional behavior: rolling in the aisles, hair pulling, fainting, or speaking in tongues. This kind of response convinces the skeptics that revivals are certainly not God-sent outpourings of new power, but are the result of deep psychological and sociological needs of the participants. The skeptics are convinced revivalists are expressing a neurotic need for ridding themselves of personal guilt by public confession, or are yielding to the power of hypnotic suggestion created by a fire-eating, stand-up-tonight-and-be-saved-preacher.

This conflict between those who strongly believe in the supernatural power of revivals and those who see it in human terms has created several difficult problems. It has

13

created sharp divisions among Christians, stretching from high denominational contests down to individual congregational squabbles. Often the bitterness created by these differences has been overcome by mutual patience and understanding. In other disputes, however, some born-again believers knew the Spirit had given them new life which could not be compromised or diluted by their staying in the old congregation or denomination. They felt called by God to create new churches where they could fully express their sense of new life. Revivalism, then, has been a very divisive issue in American Protestantism.

However, while revivalism has driven some Christians apart, it has also helped unite and strengthen others. Many revivals have brought together Christians into a common experience which they wanted to continue to share. Revivalism has brought new energy and dedication to congregations which were stale or dying. Revivals have also strengthened the faith of many who looked for concrete evidence of the presence of God in their lives.

What we have said this far, then, is that people find in revivals what they want to find: evidence of mass hysteria and neurotic behavior, or proof of God continuing to keep his promises to those who accept Christ and realize they are a "new creation."

This discussion of the conflict in the interpretation of revival is a necessary prelude. It defines the extreme positions people have taken concerning revival. These extremes should be kept in mind by the reader as he considers what the accepted understanding of authentic revivalism in America has been, and why and how the new-time religion signifies a clear break with that interpretation. So complex are the issues that it seems best to divide the book into two parts. The first, chapters 1-3, deals with the historical perspective on American revivalism to suggest why today's outpouring is so distinctive. In the second part, chapters 4-8, an analytic study is made of the important groupings within today's revival; the teen age Jesus movement, the evangelical students, the Catholic Pentecostals, and the variations of revival among the older practitioners. While some exceptions to this structure do exist, the new-time religion is most clearly perceived when studied as a religious movement whose principal groupings are defined by age levels. Those who wish to pursue the subject in more detail may find the annotated bibliography helpful.

1

THE
AMERICAN
TRADITION
OF
REVIVAL

Among the many explanations for the causes of revival, that of Professor William G. McLoughlin of Brown University recognizes both religious and political origins. He points out that the major revivals broke out primarily because of the ability of their leaders "to embody in their colorful and eloquent sermons neither more nor less than the spirit of their times." These leaders created new life and enthusiasm for the traditional "religious and secular ideals which have been the basis of the American dream." [1] The great revivalists rekindled loyalty both to evangelical Protestant teachings about sin, conversion, and regeneration, and to the respected American ideals about individual liberty and opportunity in a free land. Both the preachers and the listeners found Christianity and true Americanism inseparable.

The McLoughlin interpretation is helpful in studying American revivalism because it shows why so few outpourings turned into national movements. Hundreds of local revivals have had little or no direct relationship to American ideals. But each of the four major revivals, from the Great Awakening through that of Billy Sunday in the 1920s, has strongly identified the future of Christianity with the fate of American democracy. This union of faith and patriotism under the skilled leadership of Jonathan Edwards, Charles G. Finney, Dwight L. Moody, and Billy Sunday has elevated what might have been local movements into full-blown national revivals.

The Great Awakening

The first large-scale revival in America is still the most famous, the Great Awakening of the 1730s and 1740s. With little advance notice, revivals broke out in rural New Jersey among the Dutch Reformed churches under the inspiration of zealous itinerant preachers calling for repentance and instant conversion. At first the revivals spread rather slowly, primarily through denominational channels, in the cities and towns. Then on the frontier they accelerated rapidly with a more ecumenical and emotional flavor, reaching out to all age groups.

Much of the popularity of the Awakening depended on the eloquent preaching of George Whitefield and Jonathan Edwards. Whitefield called the sinner to recognize how far short he had fallen from fulfilling the will of God, and challenged him to think about where he would spend eternity if he did not repent. The sermons proclaimed that God had given each sinner the opportunity to trust the atonement of Jesus on the cross and to believe that once he had accepted Jesus as his savior, he would be born again. From that point he would grow through the indwelling power of the Holy Spirit to achieve a life of assurance of salvation and thus have peace with himself and his God. Out of gratitude for being released from the conviction of sin, the new believer would spend his life praising God and bringing others to this personal knowledge of salvation.

The teachings of Edwards on "eschatology" or the last things—death, judgment, resurrection, and eternal life—took on special importance for the American tradition in revival. He interpreted the biblical teachings on last things from the perspective of post-millennialism, the belief that God was creating increased improvement among people in social harmony, good will, and moral righteousness. This was the prelude to the peaceful millennium after which Christ would return for the final judgment. According to the Awakening's most knowledgeable historians, Perry Miller and Alan Heimart, this conviction led Edwards to believe that the kingdom of God would first appear in the American colonies to illuminate the way for other nations.[2] God was using revival to prepare the hearts of Americans for this great opportunity. Later revivalists, as we will see, altered this doctrine somewhat; but none of the major spokesmen rejected Edwards' linking of the future of America with the will of God.

As the Great Awakening unfolded, both its friends and critics agreed that something unusual had indeed taken place in a short time. For those who later hoped revival would come again, the Great Awakening was proof that a real outpouring could happen again. The Awakening set the standard by which future revivals would be measured.

Charles Finney and the Second Awakening

In the next decades several intense but isolated revivals broke out, mostly on the western edge of settlement. One observer at such an event in Kentucky in 1801 noted:

> Many, very many fell down as men slain in battle, and continued for hours together in an apparently breathless and motionless state, sometimes for a few moments reviving and exhibiting symptoms of life by a deep groan or piercing shriek, or by a prayer for mercy fervently uttered. After lying there for hours they obtained deliverance. The gloomy cloud that had covered their faces seemed gradually and visibly to disappear, and hope, in smiles, brightened into joy. They would rise, shouting deliverance, and then would address the surrounding multitude in language truly eloquent and impressive. With astonishment did I hear men, women, and children declaring the wonderful works of God and the glorious mysteries of the gospel." [3]

Even with such results, these revivals lacked the momentum to be expended into nationally supported revivals, primarily because they lacked unity under one strong leader. During the latter 18th and early 19th centuries several significant, but regionally based revivals broke out. However it was not until the 1830s that a powerful leader appeared, and a second national awakening broke out. Charles Grandison Finney never doubted his calling. "The Holy Spirit descended upon me in a manner that seemed to go through me, body and soul. I could feel the impression, like a wave of electricity, going through me. Indeed it seemed to come in waves and waves of liquid love. . . .It seemed like the very breath of God. I can recollect distinctly that it seemed to fan me, like immense wings." [4]

From the beginning of his career in 1822 Finney's listeners recognized how strong was his gift for conversion preaching. He moved into western New York and Ohio in the late 1820s and there established an enthusiastic following among almost all the Protestant bodies, preaching old-time conviction of sin, repentance, and instant conversion.

Finney's revivalism, however, moved far beyond the strategy used by earlier preachers. He was the first prominent figure to carry out carefully planned meetings using techniques calculated to win the maximum number of converts. Best known of these was the "anxious bench," located at the front of the auditorium for those who felt convicted of sin but not yet ready to answer the altar call. At the bench the sinner would receive intensive counseling by trained assistants. Another technique was for Finney to make public prayers for a specific individual to come forward, or often he would use "protracted meetings," which were nonstop marathons extending beyond the accepted norm of four-day revivals. Finally, he introduced planned intensive prayer meetings in private homes to help prepare a community for the coming revival. Finney also freely encouraged women to participate in all phases of a revival; this was a marked innovation for the times.

The great appeal of Finney can be understood in terms of the climate of opinion of the late 1820s and 1830s. This was the great age of "come-outer" religion in

America, when dozens of small, communal sects burst upon the scene, implementing social and economic programs which challenged the orthodox Protestants. Among the best known were the Shakers and the Mormons, both of whom presented radical alternatives to traditional religious life. Finney found his strongest support in those regions where the more radical sects were flourishing. His call for a return to the fundamentals of the faith greatly appealed to those who feared the come-outers.

Also, after several years of impressive economic growth, the nation underwent a severe depression in 1837. Finney preached that this calamity was God's judgment for man's sinful acquisition of goods, a theme which satisfied many of his listeners.

At the same time that he preached judgment, Finney proclaimed a form of Christian perfectionism, an appealing idea. He taught that by conversion and growth in sanctification the believer could approach spiritual perfection in this life. The born-again convert could learn how to restrain his sinful drives and live "in perfect obedience to the law of God." [5]

From this foundation Finney accepted the revivalist teaching that only by individual effort and personal responsibility could men cope with the many social ills of the time. Following the American tendency to glorify the self-made rugged individual, Finney preached that spiritual perfection was possible for any Christian who would reach out to take it. There were no obstacles in his way, no state church or landed aristocracy to hold him back. And when all Americans followed this command, they as a nation would be fulfilling the will of God.

Finney started to cut back on his preaching activities in

the late 1830s. Revival had swept over the land, and he thought it was now time to consolidate the gains. He had been recognized in most parts of the country as the leading preacher for the new outpouring. His success kept alive the hope that revival would surely come again.

Dwight L. Moody

Between the late 1830s and the appearance of the next great leader, American revivalism witnessed several intense but brief outpourings. Considerable interest in revival appeared during the depth of the depression of 1857; there was revival in many parts of the country, but it failed to produce a national leader to unite and direct its energy.

For the next two decades revivalism remained quiet, but then broke out in spectacular form under Dwight L. Moody, a former shoe salesman of Northfield, Massachusetts. Moody recognized the need of Americans for such a movement: anxiety and social tension developed during the depression of 1873; Protestant churches were dividing over the implications of Darwinian evolutionism; some Americans felt a new urgency to solve the crises in the urban ghettoes resulting from overcrowding, poor sanitation, crime, and the lack of formal education. These problems could be understood as proof that the American people had indeed drifted far from loyalty to God's will.

Moody was superbly equipped to understand the fears and hopes of Americans caught up in this era of transition. With little formal theological education but with an enormous talent for spellbinding revivalist preaching, he had worked his way up through YMCA and Sunday school programs in Chicago to the position of famed orator. His first real success had occurred during a revival tour of the British Isles in the late 1860s, an event he repeated in the early 1870s. By the time he was prepared to start revival crusades in America, Moody was already a celebrity worthy of front-page coverage.

From the mid 1870s through the late 1880s Moody directed the most extensive, well-organized, and publicized revival America had yet seen. He set up his crusades in large industrial cities and worked closely with the local churches. He gave special attention to cultivating the support of the local press. He set up teams of counselors and prayer circles to help create personal concern for each potential convert. He changed Finney's anxious bench into a more private "inquiry room," where the believer on the edge of decision could meditate in solitude. Yet despite his many new techniques for revival, he kept alive his simple and single-minded dedication to winning converts.

Moody preached a message which endorsed the familiar Protestant ethic of individual responsibility, hard work, personal piety, and hope for a better life in the hereafter. Although he strongly encouraged his audience to help the disadvantaged and the victims of social injustice, he carefully avoided any statement endorsing labor unions, welfare programs, or increase in government regulations of the economy. His loyalty to American ideals was based on the traditional assumption that so long as this nation followed God's will, it could do no wrong either at home or abroad. Moody fully accepted the idea that America was indeed something special in God's providence; it had a mission to extend its liberties to the less fortunate peoples of the world.[6]

With his updated methods of evangelism, his great oratorical ability, and his mastery of the common idiom, Moody became the most famous revivalist in American history. As McLoughlin suggests, a great leader reaches that peak by embodying the spirit of the times. In an era of rapid change in America, Moody preached a message which reassured his followers that neither God nor his promise of salvation had changed.

Following Moody's retirement, revivalism stayed alive and strong in the Bible institute named for him in Chicago, and in evangelical colleges, Bible schools, and seminaries across the land. But the momentum for a national outpouring disappeared when Moody left the scene, and not even the most dedicated supporter could claim between 1890 and 1910 that revival was on the land. Again the missing ingredient was a leader who could bring home to the people the need for conversion.

Enter Billy Sunday

Without much fanfare, this leader did appear in the 1910s in the person of Billy Sunday. Starting more slowly than either Finney or Moody, Sunday turned to revivalism after a brief career in professional baseball. After trying out various techniques, he developed a formula that caught on. Along with a traditional revivalist sermon on guilt, conversion, and new birth, Sunday often added to his rallies vaudeville acts, spectacular gymnastic feats on the platform, and similar razzmatazz. He also openly discussed national and world politics and the pressing social and economic questions of the moment.

Sunday's appeal can be explained largely on the basis

of the popularity of the themes in his sermons. He preached a message millions of Americans wanted to hear as they watched World War I and the Bolshevik Revolution in 1917; and with America's declaration of war they concluded with him that the Last Days were indeed here. Sunday also drew strong support for his freewheeling, sarcastic criticisms of the liberal theologians in the larger Protestant denominations. Far more bold than either Finney or Moody, Sunday delighted his crowds with wide-open attacks on bleeding hearts, do-gooders, garlic-smelling Bolsheviks, evolutionists, pinko professors, and misguided politicians. At times he considered them all of the same cloth.

Sunday knew he needed more than criticism to win converts; he needed a clear program of action for his listeners. As his antidote for the ills of the world he called for individual conviction of guilt, repentance, conversion, and new life—a message parallel to that of earlier American revivalists.

Like Moody, Sunday reassured his audiences that patriotic American ideals were harmonious with the will of God. "We are citizens of the greatest country in the world and we will admit it." Sunday considered the discovery of America along with the birth of Christ, as one of the four greatest events in world history.[7] To this he added his full endorsement of the individualistic ethic of Finney and Moody: hard work, free enterprise, suspicion of governmental regulation and welfare policies, and acceptance of monetary reward as proof of God's care. The social ills of the world and America could be mastered if each individual would be personally responsible—"Brighten the Corner Where You Are."

Sunday's flamboyance proved to be his greatest asset and liability. While it helped turn him into the most publicized revivalist in America, it could not hold the sustained interest of his followers. In the 1920s he became a nostalgic remnant. In 1933 he stated that the world would end in two years. Two years later Billy Sunday died.[8] Whereas twenty years earlier he was front-page news, now the papers were giving that space to the depression and the impending war.

2

BILLY GRAHAM
AND
AMERICAN
REVIVALISM,
1945-1960

In 1947 a young evangelist from North Carolina told a Youth for Christ audience that unless America repented from her suicidal course of crime, materialism, and godlessness, she would be destroyed in a few years. Using as evidence the rising rate of divorce, alcoholism, lawlessness, and disinterest in church activities, he called for an outpouring of the Holy Spirit the like of which Christendom had never seen before. After hinting that signs of revival were breaking out in isolated regions, he concluded: "To safeguard our democracy and preserve the true American way of life, we need, we must have a revival of genuine old-fashioned Christianity, deep, widespread, in the power of the Holy Spirit. *Our only hope is revival.*" [1]

The preacher was Billy Graham and the subject was the one which would carry him to leadership in what would be America's next revival, that of the 1950s. So decisive would that revival be in the shaping of the Jesus revival that it must be seen in some depth.

America in the Late 1940s

The momentum for revival grew out of the national frustration following World War II. Instead of being able to direct the destiny of the world as the leader of the free nations, America found its most fundamental traditions being challenged by the expansionist programs of the Soviet Union. Instead of the peace and stability dreamed of as the fruits of winning World War II, America found itself drawn into the cold war with Communists in several parts of the world.

By 1949 American citizens started demanding answers to specific questions: Why, after fifty years of world leadership should America now find itself apparently helpless to stop this atheistic dictatorship? Why, since America's goals were simply to preserve freedom and opportunity for all peoples of the world, should she now be so helpless in achieving these goals? And why were so many Americans unaware of how close they were in 1949 to having the greatness of America suddenly destroyed?

In that year, during an autumn revival in Los Angeles which had attracted little public interest in its opening days, Billy Graham attacked the complacency of those Americans who ignored the threat of Communism. He interpreted Soviet expansion as God's inevitable punishment of America for its many evils. Pointing to juvenile delinquency, crime, materialism, sexual promiscuity, gambling, cocktail bars, and political corruption as evidence of

America's galloping immorality, Graham then announced to his audience, "Russia has now exploded the atomic bomb." If the corruption from within did not destroy America, the power of the atom from without surely would.

"Do you know the area that is marked out for the enemy's first atomic bomb? New York! Secondly, Chicago; and thirdly, the city of Los Angeles!" Graham predicted all this would take place within five years unless unprecedented revival broke out in the City of the Angels and across the nation.[2]

Shortly after that prophecy, the Graham revival did become front-page news. The powerful national publisher, William Randolph Hearst, heard of the revivalist and told his Los Angeles paper to give Graham the full celebrity treatment. Soon after that, Graham received even more attention by the conversion at his crusade of several prominent Hollywood entertainment personalities. Finally, he became nationally known for the first time when Henry R. Luce, publisher of *Time* and *Life,* gave the Graham rallies extensive coverage in his magazines. It was clear that a new and dynamic force had appeared on the American revival scene.

The instant success of the Graham ministry in 1949 and early 1950 helped establish the direction for future growth: the preservation of orthodox Protestant theology and traditional American patriotic ideals by combining them into a militant revival to save both the churches and the nation. During those months the federal government made public the presence of several alleged Communist agents in the Departments of State, Treasury, and Agriculture. Graham responded: "We are told that there are over eleven hundred social sounding organizations that are communist and communist operated in this country. They control the minds of a great segment of our people, the infiltration of the left wing through both pink and red into the intellectual strata of America. Educational, religious culture is almost beyond repair—so many of our leaders feel." [3] Finding an equally perilous threat within America from the "vultures" who advocate a "debt-ridden inflationary economy with its fifteen year record of deficit finance and with its staggering national debt," Graham warned his countrymen that the churches were failing to alert their people to the peril of this crisis. Not since the Battle of Tours in 732 A.D. "has Christianity faced such an onslaught that threatens to completely wipe out all semblance of the Christian church from the earth."

In another sermon given during the same 1950 crusade in Los Angeles, Graham concluded: "We may have another year, maybe two years to work for Jesus Christ, and ladies and gentlemen, I believe it's going to be all over. *Either we shall have revival or judgment is going to fall on this nation,* and the only thing which is keeping back the judgment hand of God, tonight, is the mercy of our God." [4]

Thus, by the end of 1950 the major ingredients for a national revival had been brought back to life: an immediate threat to the nation's security, an apparent increase in immorality, and the presence of a new celebrity preacher in the mold of Finney and Moody.

Revival in the Eisenhower Era

National concern for a combined revival and counter-offensive against the Soviet Union received a tremendous boost in 1952 with the election of Dwight D. Eisenhower. Like Graham he represented a rededication to those older verities of hard work, integrity, simplicity, and personal piety. The new president often spoke publicly about his personal faith, which centered on individual responsibility for correcting the ills of America and the world. He acknowledged that his source of strength came from his prayer life and his confidence in God's personal direction of the destiny of America.With so attractive and sincere a pair of national leaders now calling for a return to the faith of the fathers, the American people joined in the new revival "for God and country."

The primary role of directing this outpouring was accepted by Billy Graham and his associates. Through carefully planned crusades in larger cities, through newspaper and magazine articles, movies, and one-stop speeches, Graham called America to repent and return to the life of righteousness and self-discipline God had intended. As his reputation here and abroad continued to grow during the mid 1950s, he decided a national revival could break out if he could carry his crusade into America's largest city, New York. After extensive consultation with local clergy he chose the spring of 1957 to launch the largest revival of his career. Although he knew Billy Sunday had called Manhattan a "graveyard for evangelists," Graham had six years of experience in mass evangelism and concluded that if the rapid decline of American morality were to be stopped, it must be done in New York.

Under the full glare of national exposure through television, radio, and the press, Graham came to New York in May for six weeks of nightly rallies in Madison Square Garden. At his first meeting he stated, "We are praying that forces will be starting here that in the next five years will make an impact on this community. I believe there is a spirit of revival in America today. I believe that history will say that 1957 was the year of spiritual awakening. I believe that God today is shaping a new generation of men and women who believe in God. I believe that the impact will be felt in days to come."

By all reports, the first meeting was a great success. Critics and cynics who had expected hair pulling, rolling in the aisles, and general hysteria were impressed with the calm devout atmosphere. And those who believed that revival was caused by the Holy Spirit rejoiced in the full house and enthusiastic reception given Graham.

For the next few weeks in the Garden, the revival went ahead with standing-room-only crowds and large numbers of converts coming forward at the nightly altar call. With such success the Graham leaders gained enough confidence to extend the rally into July. Then, with even larger crowds and continued converts appearing, they made one final extension—until the finale at Labor Day. The statistics kept by Graham's Hour of Decision staff show that in terms of the number of people attending who came forward, this revival had one of the most impressive results: of 2,397,400 who attended in person, 61,148 announced decisions for Christ.[5]

But within a year even the most ardent supporters of revival admitted that the New York Crusade had been a peak experience, and clear signs of decline in the national revival were now obvious. At first, supporters of revival suggested that after so momentous an occasion, some dropping off of enthusiasm was inevitable, and desirable. But by the end of 1958 new facts were appearing, pointing to an all-too-obvious conclusion: the revival had crested and was now slipping rapidly downward. Across the nation church attendance and new membership dropped; the sale of Bibles and religious best sellers declined, enrollment in seminaries slipped, as did new church construction. The only force for revival from the early 1950s which did not go downhill was the ministry of Billy Graham himself; that continued to hold its own.

Graham attempted to put new life back into the crusade for God and country. In a carefully thought out essay he explained what this nation had to do to recapture its ideals:

> "First, we have to recapture the spirit of individualism.
> Second, we need to recapture the spirit of '76.
> Third, we need to recapture hardness and discipline in our national life.
> Fourth, we must recapture the courage of our fathers.
> Fifth, we must recapture the American challenge.
> Sixth, we must recapture our moral strength and our faith in God." [6]

The perspective and the rhetoric of that part of the essay were familiar enough; they were standard fare for the early 1950s. But in that same essay Graham also drew up the agenda for Christian action in the 1960s. He outlined the needs of the hungry and homeless, the oppressed, and the victims of discrimination. He pointed to the worldwide problems of ignorance, disease, and poverty. He called on America to share its wealth and resources with the less fortunate of the world. Thus, for the first time in his ministry, Graham gave equal priority to pressing physical needs as well as those of the spirit.

Although no one in 1960 could have known, this

agenda was a forecast of the new issues which would concern Americans during the '60s as they turned from revival to social reform. Graham, for all his personal prestige, would not become as influential a leader in American religious life in the new decade as he had in the '50s. Like all Americans, he had some surprises in store for him as he planned to carry the "Spirit of '76" into the future. But, as it would unfold, the events of that decade were perhaps more than "surprises"; they were a shaking of the foundations in every important area of religious life. From a combination of old-fashioned revivalism, brought to life by Graham in the 1950s, and the new social activism, would come the sources for the new-time religion of the 1970s.

3

THE
TEMPESTUOUS
SIXTIES
AND THE
CHURCHES

As quickly as the revival of the 1950s disappeared from the American scene, a new and baffling set of social crises broke into public view. So critical were these problems and so fundamentally did they alter the structure of American life that we are just beginning today to understand what took place during the Tempestuous Sixties. Sydney E. Ahlstrom of Yale University suggests, "The decade of the sixties, in short, was a time when the old grounds of not only historic Western theism were awash, but also the older forms of national confidence and social idealism—not to mention traditional moral sanctions and standards of public behavior. The 1960s *did* experience a fundamental shift in the aesthetic, moral, and religious attitudes of Americans. It will probably be seen as a decisive turning point in American history." [1] The basic elements of that shift, which bear directly on the appearance of the Jesus revival, are the themes of this chapter. They center around the outbursts of protest against the status quo in four areas: civil rights, the anti-war movement, students' rights, and ecology.

The Civil Rights Struggle

The original impetus for this four-barrelled revolution came in the civil rights movement of the early 1960s. The first sign of the new black militancy appeared in the lunch counter sit-ins in 1960. Then largely under the leadership of Martin Luther King and the Southern Christian Leadership Conference, the movement for liberty and justice swept through most parts of the country. Using wade-ins, pray-ins, marches, economic boycotts, voter registration drives, and the use of television, King welded the newly inspired idealism of the white community to the renewed militancy of the blacks to press home the need for "Freedom, Now!"

The movement stirred the consciences of almost all white church groups across the nation. Northern congregations raised funds for civil rights organizations; seminary courses and programs in inner city ministry flourished; students spent vacations in the South in tutorial reading programs. A supreme moment for this coalition came in August, 1963, when in a march of two hundred thousand citizens, Dr. King gave expression to the movement with his eloquent "I Have a Dream" speech. Some months later dozens of American clergy of many denominations joined with the King movement in a march for civil rights from Selma to Montgomery, Alabama.

In the summer of 1965 the first of several major riots in black ghettos broke out in the Watts area of Los Angeles. The results were sobering; 34 persons were dead and property damage totaled more than 35 million dollars. The outbreak brought home vividly how deep and how bitter were the divisions within the black community on how to convince white America that the days of second class citizenship were over.

What worried the older coalition of white and moderate black church leaders was that continued violence would harm the cause of civil rights, perhaps beyond repair. After years of preparation, Congress had finally passed two landmark civil rights acts in 1964 and 1965, protecting equal participation in jobs, housing, public transportation, and other areas. Now this progress seemed too slow for a growing number of blacks. The new call was for a separate black community with control over its own institutions. So bitter and suspicious had many of the militants become by the mid '60s that they helped create a sense of helplessness among those holding to Dr. King's dream of black and white together. Whatever strength that movement held was lost in the smoke and ruin of the 1967 riots in Detroit and Newark, followed a year later by the assassination of King himself. The high ideals of "We Shall Overcome" seemed only a bitter memory.

The Tragedy of Vietnam

During the mid-1960s Americans found themselves stymied in another area of conflict—the war in Vietnam. Very few citizens protested the first escalation of the war by the government in Washington; it seemed to be a war much like Korea, with Communists threatening to take over all of southeast Asia. Just as America had stopped the Reds then, she would have to do it again.

But, starting on the campuses in the fall of 1965 and then spreading into churches and synagogues, a handful of critics started arguing that this was no Communist war of aggression, but a civil war between peoples of a nation in which the United States had no direct interest. During the next months both the level of American military involvement and the protest against that escalation increased rapidly. In trying to win public support for the war, the government found that it could not cope with the negative influence of television on the American public. For the first time in history, Americans daily saw the horrors of the bombing, the torture, and the refugees driven from their homes.

For reasons which will perhaps never be fully known, President Johnson could not convince the majority of Americans that world peace and American security were vitally affected by continued American participation in the war. And for the first time since the Civil War, many Americans sharply criticized their government for its war policies.

On the campuses riots broke out protesting various dimensions of the military effort: military recruiters on campus, employment recruiters from companies with war contracts, ROTC units, and campus appearances by high government officials. Quickly a new movement developed on many campuses over the issue of rights: the right to protest against those defending the war, the right of draft eligible men to refuse induction, the right of students to protest and even eliminate any military presence on campus.

As with the civil rights movement, the churches realized they must make some response to the Vietnam war. At first most spokesmen and rank-and-file members supported the government, convinced its leaders knew what they were doing in stepping up defoliation and bombing of the cities. But as the war dragged on and the American forces never turned the corner of victory promised by the Secretary of Defense, protest from individual church people was added to that of the students.

As both dissent and patriotic support for the war increased, young men turned to the churches for advice. Some of them opposed all war, but many opposed this particular conflict, and they believed that the Judaeo-Christian faith could give them direction. Many church groups and individuals responded to this need by setting up information programs and counseling services. By the end of the decade almost every organized church body had officially asked for a rapid end to the war. Only a tiny handful still called for "victory."

The anti-war movement showed a deep suspicion and fear of the policies of the national government, especially those of military security and war. Many students found themselves no longer able to support traditional American expressions of patriotism and loyalty. They wore the flag or versions of it, not out of respect but to mock it. They refused to stand for the national anthem or make the pledge of allegiance. They concluded that their government was spending over half its budget on military hardware but giving scant attention to the crucial problems of poverty and racism at home.

Thus the war in Vietnam mushroomed into a national issue far beyond the anti-draft phase, as serious as that was. During its most critical months, two more widespread crises broke out over the nation, complicating the scene even more. These were, in general terms, the "student rights" and the "ecology" movements, both of which would become very influential in the 1970s.

The Student Rights Movement

The student movement developed first at the Berkeley campus of the University of California in 1964. After some initial fumbling, its leaders settled on two major goals for their cause: making the curriculum more relevant to the solution of world problems, and giving students more authority in the decision-making processes that affected their lives.

After early success in Berkeley, the movement spread to other campuses. Often it was coupled with anti-war demonstrations; at other times it centered on abolishing rules regulating student conduct. In all but a few cases the protest movement was nonviolent but those exceptions were spectacular. At Cornell, Columbia, Wisconsin, Yale, and Harvard, to name the best-known centers, the confrontations ended with destruction of property, threats to life, and in a few tragic instances, death.

The Ecology Movement

While those under thirty were becoming embittered by what they believed was the hypocrisy of adults towards racial integration, desperate attempts to save American face in Vietnam, and indifference to student needs on campus, the ecology movement exploded. Here, the more youthful citizens concluded, was absolute proof that Americans were not practicing what they were preaching to their children. They were ruining nature's handiwork in the name of profit. They were ignoring the rights of future generations to clean air and wild flowers, pure water and green hills. Here in America, the students learned, six percent of the world's population was using up forty percent of its resources, while millions of people in the world were starving. As was true with civil rights, Vietnam, and campus turmoil, the young people found nothing in America of which to be proud.

These crises, so totally unexpected at the beginning of the decade, blended together at its conclusion to create the demand that America be turned around by one kind of revolution or another. Those under thirty refused to accept the argument that the solution to these problems would take many years of hard work and patience. The younger generation replied that unless these problems were solved at once, there was not going to be any future in which they could be solved. The appearance of that perspective marked the "fundamental shift" in the attitudes of the new generation.

The Decline of the Churches

In a final note of irony for the late 1960s, the churches, which could have been powerful institutions for direction and support of these movements, were undergoing a serious loss of strength and influence. In both the Roman Catholic Church and in the largest Protestant denominations obvious signs of decline and confusion were breaking

43

out on every level. Where once the churches seemed the most constructive leaders in the civil rights movement and in counseling those confused by the war and the draft, by 1970 most of those denominations were forced to pull back sharply on all fronts. After being told in the early '60s that they were no longer relevant to the young people, the churches plunged into relevance in the civil rights and draft movements, only to find that by the late '60s those who had been larger financial supporters were cutting back in protest. Other signs also pointed to decline: sagging attendance, slipping enrollment in seminaries, a declining market for religious books, and little parish interest for ecumenical activities like the Consultation on Church Union.

When the Gallup pollsters asked their subjects to explain this decline, the answers came back: people are changing—religion isn't important anymore—31%; the church is not meeting the needs of the people—18%, people are concentrating on other outside interests—9%; religion is no longer being taught in the home—9%. Other reasons given centered on increasing materialism, moral decay in America, and religion becoming too money-oriented.[a]

By the late 1960s it seemed apparent that American religious and secular life was moving in directions which in earlier days had led to revival. However, two crucial ingredients in the revivalist recipe were not present in 1970: a recognized leader of great popular appeal and enthusiasm for revival in a wide spectrum of age groups. Among revivalist leaders Billy Graham was still very active, to be sure. But in 1971 his ministry lacked the appeal to youth it once held. Beyond that, the polls showed that those over 30 clearly opposed radical changes in liturgy, doctrine, and social involvement of their congregations and thereby set themselves in opposition to the interests of the younger members.[3] Revivalism lacked a leader and a broad base of support.

Yet, the amazing thing about the new-time religion is that in spite of the lack of direction from the established churches, there were abundant signs of revival as early as 1969, and that in 1970 this revival was pouring out over the nation. As the next four chapters will suggest, this revival, the Jesus movement, would be a revival unique in American religious life.

4

THE
ORIGINS
OF THE
JESUS
REVIVAL

Among the questions not asked by opinion surveyors of the American public in the late 1960s was this: "Do you think the United States is on the verge of a religious revival?" The question was not asked because neither the trained observers of the religious scene nor the general public seriously believed such a thing would happen. And if the pollster had asked: "Do you think a revival might begin among counter-culture youth of California, then spread out to convert fundamentalist college students to see the social implications of the gospel, and branch out even further to include middle-class adults living in new rural communes?" the average citizen might have thought his interviewer needed medical attention. Revival watchers in America knew that authentic outpourings did not start in such unlikely sources. They also knew real revivals in America had broken out only every 40 to 50 years, and Billy Graham's crusade had passed its climax only ten years before.

But the Jesus revival would capture the loyalty of these three groups—teenagers, college youth, and adult dropouts—precisely because the "straight" world seemed so depressingly logical, orderly, and predictable. For many, Christianity in America had been systematically drained of all its joy and wonder and mystery and spontaneity. Traditional revivals with their long-range planning, their meticulous attention to the details, and their calculated efforts to get people back to the established churches had little appeal. Those caught up in the Jesus movement wanted only to follow Jesus wherever that led—into the drug culture, the urban ghetto, back to nature, or wherever. From such a conviction arose the new-time religion.

Beginnings of the Jesus Movement

Like the earlier revivals, the new-time religion emerged out of an era of grave national problems and serious self-criticism. By the late 1960s it was clear that America was not going to find fast or simple solutions to the issues of the Vietnam war, racism, pollution, poverty, or urban blight. But, as Michael Novak suggests, those who remembered the depression of 1929, World War II, the cold war, and Korea were far more resigned to accept these new crises as inevitable and beyond immediate improvement.[1] They advised their children to work patiently and obediently through the established systems of reform, rather than try to bring an instant revolution of peace and love to this world.

This proposal was unacceptable to many young people. They concluded that since the "system" had produced the disasters of war, race riots, abuse of the environment, and insensitivity to the needs of the disadvantaged, they wanted nothing to do with it. Why should they uphold free enterprise if it led only to more war, exploitation, and oppression? Why should they seek private property if it meant continuing the rat race for more materialistic goals rather than sharing with one's brother? Why, indeed, buy the American Dream if this is what it created?

Out of this rejection of the values and life style of the adult generation, the youthful dissenters started to build what became known as the counter culture.[2] More than any other single social force, this new life style would turn the Jesus revival into an outpouring much different from any earlier revival. In general the counter culture favors what the older generation is against: long hair, sloppy or bizarre dress, the use of drugs and narcotics, loud raucous music, communal living, and dabbling in Asian mystical religions.

Once having rejected the materialistic world of those over thirty, the counter culture advocates felt they were creating a whole new way of life. The primary goal was not to get ahead through competition or to measure one's worth by the standards of others. Rather, the dissident youth glorified spontaneity, feeling, and openness towards others as the means by which they could expand their inner consciousness. Instead of the nine-to-five rat-race, a home in the suburbs, and the program committee of the PTA as their goals, they wanted to prove that love, trust, and hope could turn America around from its destructive path to be again the haven of the oppressed, the land where men could start their lives over.

From the outset, the life style of the counter culture was permeated by a widespread use of drugs, from the mildest tranquilizers to the most lethal mind blowers. The promise of instant turn-on, or release from hassles with parents or teachers, or the hope for expanded consciousness through drug trips proved an irresistible lure for thousands of young people. By the late '60s the use of drugs had become a national epidemic, reaching down into the grade schools, and into the smallest towns in every part of the country.

Soon drug use was glorified by rock music, psychedelic art, and a whole new vocabulary: "blow your mind," "freak out," "drop acid," and more.[3] While the precise number of participants in this subculture can never be known, the general public believed that almost every long-haired, bell-bottomed, pro-rock teen-ager was using marijuana if not stronger stuff. Hence, the more worried and angry the older generation became over the new culture, the more rebellious and defiant those caught up in the movement became to preserve their own identity.

But the straight world was not ready to leave them alone. The police, the school officials, and the various narcotic bureaus all continued their war against the drug traffic. Such resistance was in turn regarded by the counter culture people as one more form of oppression by the Establishment.

The drug culture people in the late 1960s identified themselves with two other youth groups, the black militants and the politically activistic college students. They accepted the Black Panthers and the demonstrators at the Chicago Democratic National Convention as brothers when law enforcement agencies cracked down on them as well as on the drug users. They concluded that continued repression only helped spread their underground movement, which was being increased daily by thousands of young people who were for the first time experiencing the frustration and oppression they knew so well. There developed a loose but warm sense of companionship and empathy among all the long-haired, anti-establishment youth as they saw their elders continue the war, racism, pollution, and race for wealth.

United by a common enemy, and convinced that they alone had found the formula for peace and love, those in the counter culture continued to do their thing: no steady jobs, no contractual commitments, no participation in the formal political process, in short, nothing that would tie them to the straight world.[4] Proud to be poor and delighted by continued resistance to their morals, the people in the movement took their stand on the grounds that they alone had captured the vision of the good life.

Out of such a setting, as unlikely as it seems, the Jesus revival first took shape. It appeared first in two places, the old hippie coffee houses, where once poetry had been read but now young adults met for discussions of broader questions and, secondly, in communal houses designed to rescue drug addicts among the "street people" of Los Angeles and San Francisco. Three former drug users in their twenties, Ted Wise, Jim Doop, and Steve Heefner, with the backing of some local ministers, opened the first Christian coffee house in late 1967 in Haight-Ashbury. Naming it "The Living Room," the men and their wives welcomed teen-agers and young adults to rap with them over their problems and their religious questions. The leaders found that they were attracting those who had tried "booze, communism, anarchy, campus radicalism, and drugs." Within a few months the crowds and the need for ministering among the drug users grew so large that the leaders opened their second phase of their ministry, renting a large house in the nearby countryside to serve as a commune for those wishing to rid themselves of their addiction. Named the "House of Acts," the residence served as a half-way rehabilitation center both for its leaders, who were trying to achieve a permanent cure, and for the dozens of teen-age users who moved in and out of the house in increasingly large numbers. Although the experiment ended in 1970, the House of Acts is significant because it was the first clearly defined Jesus house in existence and set a precedent most of the later houses would follow.[5]

In 1968 much the same kind of program was created in Seattle by Linda Meissner, who had worked with teenage addicts in New York with David Wilkerson and his Teen Challenge program. Meissner became a traveling, independent revivalist in the mid 1960s, achieving some notable success with her preaching of the baptism by the Holy Spirit and the gifts of healing, tongues, and miracles. She attracted several followers out of the drug culture, and together they moved to Seattle to create the "Jesus People's Army." To the surprise of the established churches, the program of outreach to teenagers caught on quickly in Seattle and spread to Oregon and British Columbia. As with the House of Acts, this ministry focused on achieving both physical rehabilitation from addiction and the acceptance of Jesus as Savior with continued growth in the new life of discipleship.[6]

The Christian World Liberation Front

A second source of momentum for the Jesus revival was emerging in the late 1960s on the University campus at Berkeley. As the student rights movement became more militant and radical, a small group of adults working with Campus Crusade decided they must offer a viable alternative for those students who wanted to demonstrate their social concern through a Christian witness. Led by Jack Sparks, a former professor of statistics at Penn State, the organization named Christian World Liberation Front (to counterbalance the radical left Third World Liberation Front on campus) was created in 1969.

From the outset leaders of the Front carefully modeled much of its program, its language, and life style after that of the counter culture because they believed the radical students at Berkeley would not respond to a traditional church-oriented youth program. Its first public appearance came in April at one of the frequent anti-war rallies on campus, when some 200 young adults started distributing religious pamphlets and witnessing to their faith. When the larger group started a street march, the evangelists joined in, identifying themselves as the CWLF, with members carrying placards reading, "I'd Walk a Mile for Jesus," and "War the Curse—Jesus the Cure." Within a few weeks the group was publishing its own underground newspaper, *Right On,* with a style and jargon carefully modeled after that of the counter culture.

Nowhere is this better seen than in a Front's pamphlet

which shows how its program of liberation uses the concepts of the radical left, but from a Christian perspective. Replying to a tract from the revolutionary Berkeley Liberation Front which called for mobilizing the masses, the universities, and any thing else available to "destroy this racist-capitalist-imperialist system," the CWLF replied that only the transforming power of Jesus can truly meet the needs of the people. The Front found in Jesus the only person liberated from "the crippled self, the maimed world, and the scheming devil." "He will provide for the full liberation of men and women as a necessary part of the revolutionary process of building His family." [7]

This kind of message had strong appeal for teen-age and college-age students in the Bay Area. Instead of having Christianity presented to them in the traditional church-related campus programs, they found the Front leaders wearing their kind of clothes and hairdos, using their vocabulary, approving rock music—in short, taking their religion into the streets. An increasing number of them found an outlet for their religious convictions in the many-sided program of the organization. The CWLF sponsored frequent Bible raps, marches, and courses in the city's Free University. More to the point, it got directly involved in the life of the city by providing medical service for street people, distributing food and clothing to the needy, especially those in the drug culture, and maintaining several Jesus houses for those trying to kick their habit. The Front also started a summer ranch for teen-agers in the nearby mountains. Alongside that they expanded the range of interests of their paper, *Right On,* and supplemented it with a wide variety of tracts and pamphlets. The Front has also brought out its own translation of several New Testament letters, replete with counter culture jargon: "Dig it! This whole plastic bag is exactly what Jesus liberated us from." [8]

Jesus Houses Spring Up

Out of such a setting the Jesus revival emerged; it was to be a combination rescue mission, religious revival, and celebration of the life style of the counter culture all achieved far from the influence of the established churches. Following the example of the House of Acts and the Christian World Liberation Front, a dozen or so free-lance young preachers started working among the underground youth in San Francisco and Los Angeles. At the beginning, each leader would generally follow the same pattern: rent a store in the inner city; turn it into a counseling center and coffee house with free sandwiches, coffee, and Kool Aid; and invite anyone interested to stop in. During the day the preacher would spread the word that those on drugs, runaways, or others with serious personal problems were especially welcome. Most evenings the store was turned into a center for Bible discussion, group counseling and, almost always, a revival meeting. Invariably there would be plenty of group singing of old-time gospel hymns backed by either a guitar or two, or a small combo which often added some rock gospel melodies.

What made these houses different from the more traditional inner city rescue mission was, first, the heavy emphasis on appealing to teen-age street people and, second, the absence of any ties with the "straight" churches or public welfare agencies. At houses such as Arthur Blessitt's "His Place" in the midst of Sunset Strip honky-tonks, the "spaced out" drug user could find people wearing his kind of clothes and hair styles, using his language, grooving on his music, and not making any moral judgments about his habits or appearance. In fact, Blessitt used a "Toilet Party" ritual for a drug user who made a decision for Christ. As the teen-ager came forward at the call for conversion, he would be led to the toilet bowl to throw away all his pills and other drugs. Then he would return to the group for a celebration of praise and thanks to the Lord for saving him. Blessitt also used such gimmicks as "dealing reds," a phrase which referred to someone selling or giving away barbituates or "downers" which were always colored red. Blessitt, however, distributed bright red paper stickers with the name Arthur Blessitt bisected on a cross whose vertical beam formed the center of the peace symbol. Apparently no other rescue mission program on the Strip had made so bold an identification of Christianity with the drug culture.[9]

Observers of this new form of revivalism were soon wondering whether such forms of therapy had any lasting effects. Although no precise statistics are available, observers who have followed this phase of the Jesus revival are convinced that in many cases the cure from drug addiction is more than temporary. By comparison to the rehabilitation programs conducted through the major clinics and hospitals, the Jesus House programs are far more successful. One experienced evangelist to the drug culture people believes that among the 15,000 youngsters he has counseled, at least 4,000 stopped using heroin when they were born again.[10]

What struck these observers was the close parallel in ritual between the addict's decision to go clean of his habit and his decision to accept Jesus as his Savior and Lord. At the coffee house revival meetings those who had been former users would lay hands on the potential convert and pray intensely. When the drug user felt converted, he would look up at his friends. "And then the hugging begins. Unrestrained and joyous hugging, anyone, everyone. 'O God! Oh praise Jesus! Oh thank you God.'" Accepting Jesus gave the convert the supernatural power he lacked to kick his habit and join his brothers and sisters in praising God forever.[11]

To be sure, not all who attended the Bible raps or revival meetings were serious users of drugs. Many undoubtedly were "weekend street people" who could not resist the temptation to join this movement. Yet, in its original form, the Jesus movement clearly emerged out of the street people who had tried being hippies, or political radicals, or devotees of some exotic form of Asian religion or food cult.

Another close observer of this scene suggests three reasons why the drug culture people identify with Jesus.[12] First, the experience of conversion closely paralleled that of being "high" on drugs, and a deepened sense of spiritual awareness came through.

Second, both the user and the convert found in the highly simplified language of the revivalist the explanation for what had caused their trouble in the first place:

the action of the devil in this world. Both addicts and converts believed in a simple explanation of the struggle between good and evil taking place in this world; whatever is wrong is the work of the devil, and whatever is right is the work of God. Such a vision was highly popular in the entire counter culture whose spokesmen pointed to racism, war, and pollution as evidences of evil in the world.

Third, the former drug user believes that through his conversion he no longer has to face the horrors of continuing in his habit, but is now liberated to grow in the new life of following Jesus. In other words, just as large numbers of converts in earlier American revivals testified that their conversion had cured some physical ailment which medicine could not help, now the former drug user believes that his religious conversion was the only force that could enable him to kick his habit. One girl reported, "I've been saved three months. I was on dope and acid once, but now have Jesus on the inside. When I first found Jesus, I mean, it was so cool. My teacher asked if I was on something, like, you know, if I was on drugs. And I told her I had Jesus." [13]

Perhaps in such testimony lies the explanation of why the person and teaching of Jesus became so popular so quickly in such unlikely surroundings. The new-time preachers presented Jesus as a man of the street, anti-establishment, open to all sinners, loving them without expecting anything in return—patient, understanding, and gentle. Above all, the Jesus presented to the street people was a personal Savior, vitally concerned with the welfare of each individual. When Jesus' supernatural powers as exhibited in the Gospels became known to the convert, he realized he had found his Savior, friend, and liberator all in one supreme being. The kind of Jesus that the Christian World Liberation Front had proclaimed was now proclaimed among the dropouts and street people of California. Revival was on the land!

5

THE
JESUS
REVIVAL
ACROSS
THE NATION

For all of their instant popularity, the first Jesus houses open to street people could not minister to enough people to generate the revival which was soon to break out. Drug users there were in abundance, but the new-time religion was not to remain centered on that world. As news of the Jesus coffee houses and counter-culture revival meetings spread, young people without drug problems found the new movement appealing. It all seemed so "hip" or "groovy," so "now" and "with it," in comparison to traditional church youth programs.

Shortly after the success of such original programs as Blessitt's "His Place," the Christian World Liberation Front, and Linda Meissner's Jesus People's Army in Seattle, two or three dozen similar programs developed almost overnight. The southern half of California was long a natural mecca for thousands of youth who came to enjoy the warm climate, the freedom from hassles with parents or other authorities, and the adventure of the counter culture. Los Angeles and the whole Bay area of San Francisco became havens for young people who had to start over again. Here they usually were caught up in the drug culture, and in the search for the "mind-expanding" experiences they were promised in this new land of liberation.

Most of the participants in the Jesus movement came from broken or divided homes, from families where one or both parents ignored the children or gave more concern to their careers than to their children. The youth came from well-educated wealthy families rather than from any seriously disadvantaged economic class or ethnic minority. With their education and their wealth, they had found the free time to explore the full dimensions of the counter culture, which promised them so much: liberation, peace, love, God. Yet since the counter culture could not find the answers to war, racism, and self-destruction, the potential Jesus convert found no clear meaning in all his opportunities and searchings. Thus, for those who left their homes for California, there was no anchor of stability in a bewildering world.[1]

But some of them heard of the growing number of "Jesus Houses" and Christian communes which offered help, love, and direction without expecting the members to accept the demands of the straight world. They heard of mass baptisms in the Pacific ocean with personal testimonies and group singing. They heard of free rock concerts featuring groups with names like "Lost and Found,"

"Love Song," or "Everlasting Waters." They could not help but draw the parallel with the kind of community and shared love which had supposedly broken out at the Woodstock Festival. Only the new scene was freed of drugs, as the young people tried to "get high on Jesus."

In 1970, 1971, and on into 1972, the teen-age segment of the new-time religion thrived on this new understanding and living of religious faith. With several loosely organized revivalist programs to direct their new energy, youth by the hundreds started joining in the "Jesus Revolution." Alongside the drug users, a large number of part-time participants were simply curious and energetic young people who had heard of this exciting underground world and wanted to try it out for themselves.

It was this rather rapid expansion from the small rescue mission type program for addicts into mass evangelism programs that brought the movement to the attention of the national public, complete with illustrated stories in *Life, Time,* and *Look.* Suddenly, the movement took on overtones of glamor and adventure; newspaper and television reporters showed up at the ocean baptisms, and established churches quickly tried to make their own youth programs more appealing to those on the Jesus Trip.

This rapid growth of the movement was both its strength and its weakness. Its weakness at the beginning was that the enthusiastic young people were rarely given any more instruction in the Christian faith than a book of gospel tunes, a few tracts with "spiritual laws" explained with cartoons, and the assurance that once you have Jesus, everything falls into place. Teen-agers who were searching for the answers to their many questions were exposed to an explanation of Christianity which rested far more on slogans and pat answers than on encouraging youth to search out answers for themselves.[2]

Yet this rapid growth was also a sign of strength. It demonstrated that the movement was not a highly organized, mass engineered kind of revival handed out in patronizing form to young people to get them to accept the Establishment style of life. The Jesus revival among teen-agers was truly a local, grass-roots outburst, with its greatest success achieved when it shunned familiar techniques of mass evangelism and concentrated on building community. Nowhere is this better seen than in the Christian communes, or "Jesus Houses" that appeared quickly in 1969 and 1970, and kept increasing in 1971 and 1972. Each maintained its own personality, yet each shared with the others a dedication to winning converts through revival.

The Christian Communes

Following the pattern of the House of Acts, evangelists in the early months of the Jesus revival established resident houses for those trying to kick the drug habit, or recover from some family crisis or other problem. Some of these were associated with the inner city coffee houses, such as His Place; others remained independent and avoided publicity whenever possible.

With few exceptions, the general pattern of daily life in the houses is uniform. In contrast to the prevailing stereotype of the hippie, the Christian communes are kept immaculately clean outside and in. The membership runs from five to twenty-five, sometimes with an older leader as supervisor, but often with a group of young people determined to strengthen their faith in this new kind of family relationship. Every house has strict rules prohibiting sexual relations among the unmarried residents. Equally strict rules govern the use of alcohol, tobacco, any stimulants, radio, television, and other diversions. Some houses have no secular reading materials such as magazines or newspapers.

The questions most frequently asked about the Jesus communes are: what do these young people do all day? and, how is all this paid for? The answers are not always easy to obtain because many houses avoid publicity, especially about former drug users. And many houses last for only a few weeks or a few months; then the group disbands, some members returning to their families and others moving on to other communes.

However, some general patterns regarding activities and finances are apparent. The mornings are devoted to housekeeping and individual Bible study; at times this is supplemented with small-group Bible raps. In the afternoons the girls usually start witnessing and evangelizing in public—at supermarkets, on street corners, in public schools, or wherever they have the opportunity. The young men usually do their witnessing in the evenings in the same locales. The communes learned quickly that for all their trust in the goodness of people, they did not dare allow the girls out unescorted in the cities at night.

During the week the participants also spend considerable time in group discussion, usually led by the supervisor. At times these are open to the public as a means of witnessing and recruiting; at other times they are restricted to members only. At these private sessions, the members form something like an encounter group for intensive discussions of personal problems. Participants of the group offer advice as each individual pours out his feelings.

Members of the houses tell interviewers how this kind of life helps them overcome fear and loneliness.[3] They experience a sense of brotherhood based on love and joy rather than the competition and jealousy they knew in the straight world. Instead of being judged by their parents, or their teachers, or the adults of their congregations, they find in the Bible studies, prayer cells, and street witnessing a common bond of interest and concern. One of the leaders, Duane Pederson, suggests that the established churches offer the young people wall-to-wall carpeting, stained glass windows, structured programs, but "no real warmth. No changed lives. Very little honesty, no concern for the opinions and 'way of life' of others." [4]

At their houses, rock festivals, and baptisms the young people find this need filled. Having control over their own world and their own future, they find the inner resources to cope with their personal problems. Their own sense of self-esteem grows in communal living as each member encourages the others to find love and joy and to express it in worship and witness.

To outsiders this kind of living might sound dull and unchallenging—no steady employment, no clear future plans, no familiar amusements, nothing that seems "normal." But to the participants the experience opens up new opportunities for personal growth. Wanting so hard to believe in something which would fill their lives with direction and happiness, they find that by "grooving on Jesus" they are sharing the most important thing in their lives with others who had the same hang-ups and the same joy in knowing they have been saved. By a communal life which continually shows them that they have been born again and are truly saved from drugs, alcohol, fear of failing or whatever, the Jesus converts celebrate their new lives. They really believe the Bible when it says, "If any one is in Christ, he is a new creation."

In even more concrete terms, the convert rejoices in his new life because he now trusts that the Lord will provide for his every need, including food, clothing, and shelter. Adopting the counter culture's disdain for free enterprise and competitive values, the Jesus people are convinced God will give them the financial resources they need without their having to give full or even part time to regular employment. A student of the movement suggests that "God only knows" how the cash is found. Some comes from sympathetic businessmen who approve of the strict morality and no-drug regulations. Some, such as the Christian World Liberation Front, openly solicit funds through the mails. Some individual congregations support the programs of the older evangelists living in the communes. Some young people take temporary jobs such as house painting, lawn care, or snow removal. And some parents send money to their children in the movement.[5] The fact that houses do survive with such loose financial security proves to the members that God takes care of them.

A second reason for the popularity of the communes is that there is enough diversity among them to accommodate a wide variety of religious life styles. As the movement expanded from rescue missions into broader evangelistic work, the kinds and numbers of communes and coffee houses increased. Although precise numbers are unavailable, by the end of 1971 some two hundred Jesus houses were in operation on the West Coast, and perhaps a comparable number in the rest of the country. Among the more publicized houses with special interests were the Lord's Fish House in La Mesa, California, opened for former motorcycle drivers; Bethel Tabernacle in Redondo Beach ministering to users of hard drugs; Solid Rock House in Novato reaching out to unwed mothers; and Koinonia Community of Santa Cruz sheltering those on legal probation.

One of the most highly publicized communes with a charismatic emphasis is the Christian Foundation of Saugus, California, directed by Susan and Tony Alamo. At one meeting an observer found two hundred young people participating "with wildly gyrating bodies," singing old-time gospel hymns, giving personal testimonies and prayers. He concluded: "Never have I seen such energy, such fervor, such body-and-soul enthusiasm spent on religious worship. They were on the edge of hysteria the entire time. Arms lifted heavenward, feet stamping, all stops pulled, they screeched song lyrics unto God, moaned and groaned, shuddered and had fits." [6]

For those wanting something more sedate, there was the JC Light and Power House near the UCLA campus, which placed more emphasis on group discussion and Bible study, with a heavy premillennial accent. Most of the residents either attend school or hold a steady job and pay a specific amount to the House for room and board. The enthusiasm there was more subdued, and the general tone of the commune more reflective. [7]

In an older section of Los Angeles are the offices of the *Hollywood Free Paper* and Emporium directed by

Duane Pederson. The newspaper itself had a circulation of some 500,000 by the end of 1971 and served as a clearing house about Jesus revival activities in all fifty states. In the classified sections were listed programs and activities of a wide variety of Jesus movement people along with addresses and telephone numbers for further information. The paper, which looks like a counter culture underground publication, also presented brief sermons, testimonies, Bible lessons, and cartoons. The Emporium was the supermarket of the organization, selling Jesus posters, bumper stickers, tee shirts, jewelry, tracts, pamphlets, and other memorabilia. All profits went to the evangelistic work of the paper. Pederson himself toured the nation in revivalistic crusades to create new support for the program.

By mid-1972 dozens of comparable urban communes had emerged in most of the nation's largest cities and in several Canadian towns. These have received comparably little national publicity, and for the most part their members prefer to remain anonymous. Some denominational programs centering on social service have attempted to open similar rehabilitation houses under the supervision of trained clergymen. Among the better known is the Renewal House in Los Angeles, supported by Lutheran Social Services. The denominations have found the need but not the adequate resources to expand on this ministry.[8]

Another variation appeared in Houston, Texas, under the dynamic leadership of John Bisagno, pastor of the First Baptist Church. He worked out a blend of Jesus revival meetings—with rock music, mass baptisms, and intensive personal witnessing—and his own youth program in the congregation. Much of the success for the program came from a well-organized revival program called SPIRENO—Spiritual Revolution Now!—created by a 25-year-old touring evangelist, Richard Hogue. Using an easy-rock trio, he had already created wide interest in Jesus circles by smaller scale programs in schools and in public programs. In every case he made an altar call, and invariably nearly half of the teen-age audience would come forward. Under Bisagno's sponsorship, SPIRENO produced an all-out evangelistic blitz of Houston for three months with music-testimonial programs in the junior and senior high schools, evening programs in the churches, and appearances on the city's radio stations. At the end of the three-month program Bisagno estimated that of the 11,000 teen-agers who registered decisions for Jesus, some 4,000 of those were genuine conversions.[9]

Other variations of both independent and church-related youth programs quickly followed. Some, such as Lutheran Youth Alive, provided a format of one- or two-day Jesus festivals with music, preaching, testimonials, and calls for conversion. Most of these variations reached out for all teen-agers, not simply those caught up in the drug culture or with other intense emotional problems. Success was not always assured for these programs; some festivals only attracted a small number of participants. Yet, for all their variety, these alternatives shared one major theme with the original Jesus revivals in California: they all celebrated the life and joy and love that was the reward for those who followed Jesus. The outpouring of enthusiasm was, and is, in the traditional American revival pattern. What a Jesus person knows is that "when you love Jesus, it all comes together."

The Teachings of the Jesus Revival

Once a young person has answered the altar call he is faced with the question: what is God's will for my life now? The convert faces the need for studying the Bible, listening to his leader, and rapping with others to understand more clearly how Jesus can be his Lord and Savior. In other words, he must learn something about the teachings of Christianity for the sake of his own life and also to witness to non-believers.

The question becomes for the observer: what do the Jesus people believe? One qualifying note must be made at the outset. The young people have had little time or opportunity for any extended study of theological issues, and therefore they accept teachings that seem to harmonize with their personal experience of trust in Jesus even though such teachings may be superficial and easy to refute. That qualification would not particularly bother a Jesus follower, however. He knows he has been saved and no "head trip" or logical analysis of theology could challenge that knowledge.

The first thing he has come to know and experience is the release from guilt and loneliness he knew before conversion. That transformation came about when he accepted Jesus into his life. Nothing is more clear to him than that. One writer says: "Jesus is the most exciting and loving Person who has ever lived. The way that He loves is not plastic. It is not a fabrication of the establishment. It isn't pumped with speed, and it isn't just positive thinking! It is for real and it fulfills. It is, in fact, the only thing that does. On the basis of the kind of life Jesus lived and the liberation He gave and continues to give to people, do you think you could trust Him with your life? *Can you think of any man you'd rather follow?"* [10]

The convert learns that the best source of knowledge about Jesus is the Bible. With but few exceptions, the Jesus people accept the traditional American revivalist doctrine that the Bible is the inerrant, infallible, verbally inspired Word of God. Like Moody, Sunday, Graham and the others, the leaders of the revival tell their followers: "If there is one error in the Bible, there are millions of them." This satisfies the converts, and they study and memorize huge portions of Scripture, looking always for the literal meaning of every passage. Further, they are taught to believe in the "topical" method of exegesis. That is, the Bible is so perfectly and harmoniously constructed that the reader can move with full confidence from one book to another in studying, for instance, "love" or "justice" and see how it all fits together. According to the Jesus people God did not intend that the Bible be difficult or the property of trained scholars. He planned that every true believer with Jesus in his heart can understand the Bible and how it should be applied to his life. Every answer to every question is to be found there if believers trust God to show them the answer. [11]

In studying the Bible, the new believer learns to imitate Jesus wherever possible. He is taught that for centuries earlier Christians have imitated Jesus in two specific ceremonies, baptism and communion. Jesus converts in California participated in baptism by total immersion in the Pacific or in the pool on the Berkeley campus, or wherever a body of water was available. The believer understands the ceremony is a physical enactment of his decision to wash away his sins and to join with his brothers and sisters in the new brotherhood of followers. At most of the mass baptism ceremonies an informal communion ceremony followed the immersions. With little prior explanation or ritual, some leaders would distribute either grape juice or wine in a common cup with crackers, saying, "This represents the body of Christ broken for you" or "Jesus shed his blood on the cross for you." [12] Rather than teaching that the baptism and communion are sacraments of the historic Christian faith, the leaders explain them as means of celebrating together the oneness and freedom that is God's "forever" family.

The Jesus follower believes he has within him new, supernatural power he had never known before. He learns from others that this too is a part of God's plan of salvation for him because it means he has come to know the Holy Spirit. The teaching about the third person of the Trinity is not anywhere nearly as precise among Jesus people as those concerning Jesus, the Bible, and conversion. Yet, despite this vagueness, each believer comes to understand he feels blessed because the Holy Spirit has come into his life. He is taught by his elders the Spirit does not "turn on" every believer in precisely the same way. As a result, some differences do appear, a fact which may confuse the outside observer, but only convinces the believer that the Spirit does indeed move in many ways.

The complexity of this teaching appears to the convert when he understands that when the Holy Spirit comes into his life in the manner of the events on the first Pentecost, that event can bestow on him certain gifts which he never possessed before.[13] He may come to have powers of healing, or he may speak in tongues, or be able to interpret the language of those who do speak in tongues. He may be given the power of prophecy or of greater wisdom. He may receive all of these gifts or only one of them. But he understands this much about the teaching on the Holy Spirit: his life has new supernatural powers it never had before, and he is to use these powers to the glory of God.[14]

A final major teaching shared by almost all Jesus people is that regarding the Last Things—death, judgment, resurrection, eternal life. The converts learn quickly they must expect the imminent destruction of this planet; as wars, weapons, pollution, racism, earthquakes, forest fires, and degeneracy grow worse, it becomes evident that nothing less than the literal second coming of Jesus can preserve the true believers from destruction. As men and nations seek to preserve themselves by such man-made schemes as the welfare state, socialism, atomic bombs, armies, and all the rest, they are only showing how far from faith in God's providence they have moved. Man can do nothing to save himself from destruction, and soon Jesus himself will come to prove that once and for all.

The appearance of this teaching among Jesus people shows that in this instance the new-time religion depends on the old-time doctrines of the Last Things. Many readers will recognize the Jesus people position as traditional apocalyptic premillennialism now updated to include such things as the nuclear weapons, the Jews returning to their homeland, and the rise of Red China. Hal Lindsay, of the JC Light and Power House in Los Angeles, has written what has become a major text of the Jesus movement, *The Late Great Planet Earth* to demonstrate that the last days are here.[15] Speaking to a generation reared on a diet of science fiction, atomic bombs, and global pollution, Lindsay shows how the "signs of the times" prove Jesus is coming. The teen-agers find this fact not frightening, but immensely reassuring. To them it is the final proof, beyond human wisdom or logic, that the Bible must be literally true. God is living up to the time-table he wrote into the Bible; unless men accept that simple fact, they will soon be destroyed.

Undoubtedly, the virtually unanimous acceptance by the converts of this understanding of the end of the world helps explain why they have rejected the heavy political activism of the youth of the late 1960s, and instead cry "Maranatha—he is coming." That conclusion, so characteristic of the earlier great revivals in American history, leads the Jesus follower to accept a rather clear-cut set of doctrines concerning his relations to his fellow residents on this planet.

The Social Ethics of the Movement

Other than in life style, the sharpest break between traditionalist revivalist teachings and today's Jesus revival among teen-agers (but not college students, see Chapter 6) is in their differing interpretations of social ethics, of how Christians are to express their faith in relation to society. The break is so sharp and so clearly related to the appeal of the new left counter culture that it makes this revival one of a kind. Jonathan Edwards, Charles Finney, Dwight L. Moody, Billy Sunday, and Billy Graham did not show any inclination to disparage private property or ignore patriotic loyalty to the nation. These, however, are commonplace convictions of the Jesus followers, convictions that make their revival unique.

The Jesus converts accept the counter culture attitude toward both private property and patriotism. They reject the idea that the accumulation of private property is a just reward for hard, law-abiding work. The young people find the churches too busy taking care of property to take care of souls. They find their parents or elders too caught up in the destructive pleasures that wealth can buy: entertainment, liquor, creature comforts, status symbols such as boats or big cars.

The Jesus people turn instead to the commune as the only biblical form of community to overcome the temptations of private property. By sharing all their possessions they are proving how far they are willing to trust God to provide for them. Like the early Christians, they want to sell their property and share all things in common. No concept of personal property could be further from the convictions of Moody, Sunday, or Graham.

In the area of patriotism and war, the social ethics of the Jesus revival also follows that of the new left counter culture rather than traditional revivalism. In general the Jesus converts do not support the war in Vietnam, and indeed, they encourage resistance to the draft. In their public marches, for instance, they display placards reading, "Would Jesus Carry a Draft Card?" or "Get Out Now." A popular poster in the movement in "Stop Work! Stop War!" One of the most distinguished evangelical scholars in America, Carl F.H. Henry, who shows great enthusiasm for the Jesus movement, admits that "some of the evangelical hippies—often as a reflection of their discontent concerning Vietnam—refuse to salute the flag." [16] In brief, the traditional forms of patriotism and loyalty, so cherished by Moody, Sunday, and Graham, leave the Jesus kids bored and unimpressed.

With the exception of the Christian World Liberation Front, the Jesus converts show little or no interest in political activity. One minister, after interviewing a new member, reported that when he asked her about the implications of the Gospel for racial justice, poverty, or pollution, she replied, "Oh, they're bad. But the main thing is to love Jesus."

Such sentiments abound in the movement. This outlook, as suggested above, is the natural outcome of the premillennial teaching that nothing worthwhile in society can be achieved in this life, that for biblical prophecy to be fulfilled, evil and sin must increase in this world.

Further, this indifference to collective ills suggests how deeply some Jesus converts resent the highly activistic social involvement of many of the established churches. To them, the churches are cold, sterile, and hypocritical; they have not cleansed the world of hate. So the new believers join in groups which deliberately reject the programs of the established churches. They accept the fatalistic position that this world is headed towards destruction. In answer to their activist critics who want more social involvement, they state that since Jesus could save sinners like themselves, he can if he wants to also save this world without the help of man. It's all up to Jesus.[17]

Thus, out of the drug culture of California and the rapid growth of the counter culture emerged the beginnings of the teen-age version of the new-time religion. Much of its vocabulary was that of earlier revivals, but its social ethics was something new in American religious life.

6

THE
NEW
CAMPUS
COMMITMENT

The new-time revival in America shows signs of developing into a major outpouring largely because it embraces a wide variety of age and interest groups. Just as the Jesus movement appeals to teen-agers, a renewed sense of the presence of the Holy Spirit is producing a strong commitment of faith from college students and seminarians. With some exceptions, this new movement also draws heavily on the life style of the counter culture.

The mood on American campuses in the early 1970s shows a clean break with the temper and spirit of the '60s, when the campuses changed from isolated ivory towers to centers for militant activism of all kinds. During the height of campus protest movements two major demands emerged: a curriculum more relevant to the problems of society, and much stronger student authority in helping make the policies of the campus community. Caught up in the idealism of young adult life the students wanted to transform their campuses into communities of personal commitment from which a better society could be formed.

At many schools this new concern revitalized the campus ministry programs of the major denominations. The leaders and students wanted to study more closely the problems of war, racism, and pollution, and learn what they could do to relate their faith to such concerns. Many campus ministries became centers for anti-war and anti-draft teach-ins, for seminars on drugs, sexuality, the new theologies, and racism. So popular were some of these programs that they attracted national notice through the bold leadership of men like William Sloane Coffin of Yale or Daniel Berrigan of Cornell. Even the critics of these men admitted that more students were attending church services led by such men than ever before. The students found that this kind of Christian organization related directly to their immediate concerns.

However, while this momentum was increasing, the national polls showed a decisive decline of student interest in the established denominational church programs. The students' bill of complaints was long: too much bureaucracy, too much red tape, and not enough boldness to support experimental ministries such as to drug addicts. The students objected to the tone of "niceness" and gentility exuded by well-dressed middle-class parishioners who were repelled by the long-haired dissidents. They objected to denominations keeping traditional church body lines drawn firmly rather than experimenting with ecumenical programs. And they faulted the churches for not speaking out boldly on the major issues of the day when a Christian witness was so deeply needed. In general, the students agreed that American society was too up-tight, too materialistic, too afraid to change, and too timid to trust and love people without thought of personal risk.[1]

To sum up, recognizing the depth of the crisis facing America in the late 1960s but finding no reason to think the organized churches would be able to minister to these problems, college students who were searching for authentic religious insight started looking outside traditional organizations for leadership and encouragement. Like the Jesus followers, they too would believe that a true revival had broken out alongside rather than inside the churches. And, like the counter culture, the campus revival would show both diversity and unity, the unity centered on the need of the participants for liberation from the establishment to give them the personal freedom they needed for growth and service.

Revival Time

In contrast to the days of marching, protest, and dissent of the late 1960s, several American campuses in the early 1970s became caught up in revivalism. A staff psychiatrist at Harvard, Dr. Armand M. Nicholi, told a conference of colleagues that he had seen the lives of many students "changed from completely secular life style to a full commitment to Christ." [2] He found the students' "intensive social concerns have by no means diminished, but their method of expressing these concerns have altered quite radically." In 1971 at Rensselaer Polytechnic Institute, not famous for its evangelical concern, a two-day festival for "turning on to Jesus" was zestfully attended by some four thousand students, nuns, ministers, and Jesus people. Easily the most spectacular outpouring of all happened at Asbury College, Wilmoore, Kentucky, in February, 1970. Without warning, a spontaneous marathon revival broke out among both students and faculty. Classes were cancelled for a week during the chapel services, which continued non-stop for 185 hours. The participants freely confessed their sins and came forward for forgiveness and rebirth in the Holy Spirit. Those who participated and those who observed were convinced it was an authentic revival.

So caught up with enthusiasm were the students and faculty that several left Asbury to bring news and a witness to other campuses and churches wherever they were invited. Smaller but fervent revival meetings developed on a dozen evangelical campuses. A year later, when the event was summarized by Asbury faculty members in a book, *One Divine Moment,* the participants and observers found the campus more quiet but inspired by a strong sense of renewal and personal commitment.[3]

The follow-up revivals on campuses across the nation did not turn into full-fledged outpourings, as many believers had so fervently hoped. Instead, the most marked and significant changes among the Protestant evangelical student groups appeared in 1970 and 1971 in the form of far deeper involvement in social and political issues. While in 1947 Carl F. H. Henry chided evangelical students for showing more interest in whether to allow the playing of Rook than in public questions, in 1970 the same students were enthusiastically debating everything from abortion to draft resistance to marijuana.

This transformation was remarkable because of the

long-standing opposition to strong involvement in social issues by elders in their churches. Now, under the full glare of mass media exposure and the upheavals on the nation's campuses, this group of Christian students absorbed the concerns for social issues expressed by the new left counter culture into their own understanding of religious faith. A close look at the three principle student organizations caught up in this phase of the new-time religion will show how far the participants have come from the social concerns of their revivalist ancestors.

The American Association of Evangelical Students

The first of these is the American Association of Evangelical Students (AAES), which in 1969 found delegates to its annual convention bored with the traditional agenda on methods of personal evangelism. The leaders decided to emphasize social involvement at the next convention. In the spring of 1970 some two hundred AAES delegates devoted most of the three-day meeting to discussing the nation's most pressing questions. Spirited debate broke out over the means by which racial prejudice could be reduced on their own campuses; at the same time the delegates rejected the demands of James Foreman for reparations payments. The students called for greater study of population problems, contraception, and related issues. They called on members, when married, to limit their families to two children or to adopt orphans. On campus issues, the delegates called for extensive student evaluation of teachers and administrators and for student representation on standing committees and boards of trustees.

During the convention considerable criticism was voiced

about the institutional churches: their irrelevance, their avoidance of social issues, their suspicion of young adults with counter culture wardrobes and hair styles. The students narrowly approved a motion condemning the American invasion of Cambodia.[4] Five years before, or perhaps even two years before, such issues would not have been on the agenda of the American Association of Evangelical Students convention.

In their 1971 convention, the delegates of AAES, meeting at Oral Roberts University, moved even farther into the mainstream of the new-time religion.They invited a well-known Roman Catholic Pentecostal leader, Kevin Ranaghan, to address them, knowing many of their parents and elders still considered Catholics to be anti-American. The students had a long discussion with members of the Children of God group and with young new left political leaders. In short, the delegates wanted to learn what and where the action was outside their own campuses. For the first time they debated whether to allow students from secular campuses to join AAES; the motion carried, and the Association found itself a new kind of organization.

When the social issues were taken up, the delegates gave them serious consideration. One resolution calling abortion "murder" was defeated badly; a resolution asking for abolition of capital punishment carried by a 3 to 2 margin. Other resolutions approved called for a ban on DDT, for strong revisions of the Selective Service System to prevent forcing upon draftees "participation in immoral wars. . . contrary to principles of Christian love." Several resolutions criticized the timidity and stiffness of established denominational social action programs; one resolution asked for the "relaxing of penalties against marijuana users," but did not condone its use. As a finale, and evidence of their social concern, the delegates elected a woman as president of AAES.[5]

Inter-Varsity Christian Fellowship

The second group and the largest and most representative national student group to reflect the impact of the new-time religion is the Inter-Varsity Christian Fellowship. The new concern for social ills came strongly to the surface at the triennial convention in Urbana, Illinois, in December, 1970. Traditionally the IVCF meetings had attracted students from denominational and Bible colleges who were primarily interested in foreign mission work. The meetings had always been lively, well-attended, and very much a part of the established denominational scene. However, in 1970, with 12,300 students in attendance, the meeting would prove to be "something else."

As the delegates gathered at Urbana for the first time in three years, the most visible signs of change became clear. Many of the students had adopted the dress of the counter culture: bell bottoms, minis and maxis, bright colors, beards for the men, waist-length hair for the women. The most popular music was "God-rock" and black soul music performed by groups with names such as "Soul Liberation." They did not play "In the Garden" or "Kumbaya." Not even "Jacob's Ladder."

Among the main speakers the black revivalist, Tom Skinner, received the greatest approval. This response is of the greatest importance for understanding the new currents in the student movement. In earlier years the delegates had listened to famous professors, celebrity preachers, or prominent athletes discuss the Christian life. In 1970, however, the students turned to Skinner, a former Harlem gang leader, knowledgeable in the world of drug culture and crime, and made him their spokesman. They repeatedly stood and cheered his blistering attacks on the complacency and hypocrisy of middle-class American life, with special criticism for its stodgy, lifeless churches. Skinner's preeminence was recognized also by the adult leaders of IVCF, one writing that the evangelist "epitomized the spirit that prevailed throughout the four-day conference." [6]

Skinner demonstrated with devastating personal illustrations how the churches contributed to institutionalized racial discrimination and poverty. He went on to show that the evil in this world was not going to be overcome by waiting for the Second Coming or by trying to deal with social problems on a one-to-one personal basis. Repeatedly, the Inter-Varsity students cheered his criticism of such basic national institutions as Wall Street, big business, the bliss of suburbia, and what he called the "myth of democracy."

So far Skinner's message would harmonize with the indictments of the new left counter culture. However, rather than join that movement in calling for political change, Skinner presented Jesus to the student as the only liberator from oppression. Drawing on the jargon and the imagery of the new left, Skinner told the delegates Jesus was the only force for change powerful enough to save humanity from destroying itself. Revolution, he stated, was not the kind of political rebellion carried on by secular forces. Revolution was "allowing the common clay of your humanity to be saturated with the deity of Christ and for you to go out into open display as a living testimonial that it is possible for the invisible God to make Himself visible in a man."

He charged the Inter-Varsity listeners to become truly radical by becoming "part of that new order and then go into a world that is enslaved, a world that is filled with hunger and poverty and racism and all those things of the work of the devil. Proclaim liberation to the captives, preach sight to the blind, set at liberty them that are bruised, go into the world and tell men that are bound mentally, spiritually and physically, *'The liberator has come.'* " [7]

The Skinner phenomenon at Urbana shows how far this student group is from the stereotype of the anti-intellectual fundamentalist indifferent to social issues. Because of the impact of the counter culture on the campuses, this phase of the new-time religion is in the best sense a revival. It demands that the participants break cleanly with earlier hangups about keeping the churches out of social action, and it is leading many of the students to express their faith by working in urban ghettoes, in the drug and crime subcultures, and in rural poverty areas.

In other words, these college students accept Skinner's claim that certain basic national institutions are as responsible for the evil and misery of this world as is personal sin; they accept the counter culture's rejection of middle class values, materialism, and lack of social concern. Like the Jesus people the students embrace Jesus as the liberator from such stagnation and oppression and as the Lord who leads them into making the system sensitive to his teachings of brotherhood and love. According to a member of the Yale Religions Ministry program, the students find in

Jesus a person who was able to express a wide variety of life-roles. "Depending on the orientation of the individual, Jesus might become a model for the Socratic Teacher, Drop-out Carpenter, Prototype of Civil Disobedience, Liberator of his People, Mystery Man, Moral Authority, Faith Healer or Communal Organizer." [8] Earlier revivalist spokesmen in America would not have shared that conviction.

Campus Crusade for Christ

Like the other student groups, the Campus Crusade for Christ believes that an authentic revival is breaking out over America, giving it the greatest opportunity in its history for winning souls for Christ. In accord with the popularity of very large gatherings among young adults, the Crusade in late December, 1970, sponsored six rallies across the country. During the discussions on ethics, the delegates gave no serious attention to the earlier understanding of sin as personal wrong doing—such as smoking, drinking, dancing, card playing—but focused sharply on institutional ills. They explored the complexities of finding a "Christian position" on such issues as violence, drugs, war, racism, poverty, pollution, materialism, sexual immorality, and false religion.

At the conventions the delegates for the most part accepted the charge that the churches and campuses had failed to come to terms with these problems. Believing, though, that an outpouring of power in the Holy Spirit is available to each of them, the Campus Crusade mobilized in late 1970 for an all-out evangelism blitz. They have continued to use several means of witness, primarily personal visits with potential members on campuses and distribution of tracts wherever students meet, including Woodstock and the Florida beaches, along with leadership training institutes and musical programs with revivalist overtones.[9]

During the eight regional meetings it sponsored in late 1971, Campus Crusade identified itself closely with the general Jesus revival. After some training in evangelistic witnessing techniques, the students hit the streets, in the fashion of the Jesus people, to win decisions for Christ.[10]

Other Campus Revival

In the spring of 1972 the momentum for revival on campus continued to grow. Students at such former hot-beds of new leftism as Santa Barbara showed sustained interest in the Jesus movement. A chaplain at the State University of New York at Albany reported strong interest from Catholic, Jewish, and Protestant students in evangelistic coffee houses, cell groups, and Bible study. Similar interest appeared growing at Princeton and Harvard.

What appeared to be something close to authentic revivals were emerging at two campuses, Eastern Illinois University at Charleston and North Park College in Chicago. In both instances large numbers of students joined in informal discussions and testimony sessions. With no advanced planning or concern for statistics, the adult leaders of these outpourings found the students willing to acknowledge their sins publicly and to answer the altar call spontaneously and informally.[11]

The increasing enthusiasm on campuses for AAES, IVCF, Campus Crusade and related evangelism activity is expressed further in the appearance in recent years of many, little-known, deliberately small campus renewal bodies. Some of these have official denominational sponsorship; others have loose ties with the churches or campus ministries, and some are determined free lancers. Of special interest is the fact that almost all Protestant groups are represented in the college expression of the Jesus revival. Every Protestant body with more than 100,000 members has some newly revised and energetic evangelism program on campus. In almost every case the student participants are far more interested in reaching out to help the victims of social oppression and in communicating with fellow students than they are in maintaining any kind of strong denominational loyalty. At week-end retreats, summer camps, and cell meetings, the young adults find that older barriers of doctrine and church practice fade into obscurity as they share their faith with one another. Some of these discussions have broken down, but more often than not the participants find they all share the same allegiance to Jesus and to revival.[12]

Speaking in Tongues

Alongside this genuine ecumenicity, the student revival today stands sharply divided—as does the larger Christian community—over the explosive issue of speaking in tongues, or glossolalia. One reason contributing to the popularity of the small and independent campus groups is that many stress "baptism of the Holy Spirit" and spiritual gifts like tongues and faith healing. Neither the AAES nor Inter-Varsity or Campus Crusade recognizes this phase of the spiritual life as being essential to personal growth.

As a result, those who wish to follow this phase of the revival generally work in small groups.

Among those associations which actively seek national student support is Campus Fellowship, headquartered in Waco, Texas, with branches across the country. It does not make tongues the central theme of its ministry, but it does teach that supernatural gifts of the Holy Spirit are given to believers today as they were in the early church. Interestingly enough, some of its strongest supporters are rehabilitated drug addicts, who found warmth and acceptance in this movement. One college girl from a small town in western Minnesota gave her testimony:

> I honestly expected grass to be the answer—it wasn't. Within two weeks I was taking LSD. I remained stoned day and night and began to lose all sense of reality. I got lost in myself. I sold myself to the needle and cared about little else. I say my friend going through heroin withdrawals, yet one week later I told her I didn't care if I became addicted.

She attended a summer conference of Campus Fellowship near Waco, "Just to get away for awhile."

> The Lord had different plans. He dealt with my heart quite severely at Waco, and so did the Devil. I went through two days of constant battle. Praise the Lord, He won. I got down on my knees, sobbing, and asked the Lord Jesus to forgive me and take over from now on. My tears turned to tears of joy as I felt His loving hand touch me. The next day I was baptized in the Holy Spirit. The feeling I had when the Holy Spirit came upon me was stronger than a heroin rush. . . . I just kept getting fuller of joy." [13]

In other respects, the teachings of Campus Fellowship closely follow those of traditional Protestant fundamentalism with its individualistic ethic, its belief in instant conversion, followed by growth in sanctification, and in the apocalyptic premillennial understanding of the future. However, no apparent rapport is being achieved between the tongues faction and its critics. Within each of these groups, however, there is a sense of community and acceptance, and members fear any larger involvement would weaken their oneness in the Spirit.

The Catholic Pentecostals

One of the impressive features of the new-time revival on campus is its ecumenical nature. The revival is so strong today and so much a break from earlier revivals, that in its Pentecostal dimension, it is embracing also Roman Catholics. That development would not have happened in earlier outpourings. Generally these Catholic groups want to remain Roman Catholic and to explore the full range of religious consciousness they find opened to them through the baptism of the Spirit. Out of this is slowly emerging something most remarkable: Protestants and Catholics are no longer trying to convert one another to the true faith, but are sharing the excitement and renewal they have experienced.

Among the many dramatic and far-reaching transformations within American Roman Catholicism in recent years, none reflects more fully the impact of the new revival than this "charismatic renewal." Its supporters are fully convinced that an authentic revival is sweeping across the country. By the end of 1971 Catholic Pentecostalism embraced between 10,000 and 50,000 believers, located mostly in college communities.[14]

In contrast to the teen-age Jesus movement and the rural commune phenomenon, this phase of the revival is more concerned with formal theological doctrine, precise study, and with involvement with the established churches. As early as 1969 an official policy statement by the National Conference of Catholic Bishops pointed out that this renewal is disassociated from "classic Pentecostalism as it appears in Protestant denominations, such as the Assemblies of God, the United Pentecostal Church, and others. The Pentecostal movement in the Catholic Church . . . likes to consider itself a renewal in the spirit of the first Pentecost." [15]

That insight by the bishops points to the unique feature of this revival, its close attention to doctrine. As the movement first appeared, at a spiritual retreat in 1967 in Duquesne University in Pittsburgh, its leaders were attempting to restore life and reform within the church. It quickly spread to other campuses, emphasizing renewal as the result of the baptism in the Holy Spirit with the charismatic gifts of the New Testament. These gifts, as one leader suggests, "are poured out on a group of believers for the sake of building up the Church and for the purpose of facilitating the proclamation of the Gospel. They are simply tools for the body of Christ. A charism is a gift given for the common good. The specific spiritual gifts that seem to be most in evidence in this charismatic renewal, in this outpouring of the Spirit, are those listed in 1 Corinthians 12 by St. Paul; words of wisdom, knowledge, faith, healing, miracles, prophecy, discernment, speaking in tongues, and interpretation of tongues." [16]

However, it must be added here that these nine charisms are not by any means the only gifts bestowed on

93

the believer by the baptism of the Holy Spirit. One of the most penetrating theologians of the movement, Donald L. Gelpi, S. J., points out that the charismatic experience is expressed in several spiritual gifts given for the benefit of all, that some gifts are larger than others and that "no complete catalogue" can be drawn up listing all of the gifts. The believer knows rather that the Spirit "apportions his gifts according to each individual's needs and the needs of the community." [17]

Like the Jesus people, the Catholic Pentecostals believe that American church life has become so formal and cold that it no longer fills the promise of Christ to make all things new. The Catholic Pentecostals want to recapture the excitement of the first Christians at Pentecost. They believe that by following the indwelling power of the Holy Spirit, as did those first converts in Jerusalem, they can transform their own lives, those of their community and, hopefully, the entire Roman Catholic Church.

What has happened since 1967 shows clearly both the strengths and limitations of this phase of the new-time revival. The news of the Duquesne outpouring quickly spread to other campuses and seminaries. Quietly at first, and then more dramatically, the movement attracted growing numbers of younger priests, nuns, seminarians, and students on or near campuses; they began to explore the possibilities of renewal for themselves. Through small cell groups, mid-week prayer meetings, and regional conferences, many found a new spiritual life by receiving the gifts of the Holy Spirit. While bitterness and confusion swept through American Catholicism concerning the changes after Vatican II in education, the mass, and other areas, those caught up in the charismatic renewal found inner resources for stability and dedication to share these gifts with others. They understood their ministry as a call for rededication to the vision of the early church, where love and community prevailed over the clamor of disputes.

Such a vision in the late 1960s greatly appealed to younger Catholics, especially those with more advanced academic education. Those receiving the baptism of the Holy Spirit carried their gifts to other college communities such as Ann Arbor, East Lansing, and Grand Rapids. By late 1970 the movement had spread out from the campus into dozens of other cities, not attracting large numbers but establishing itself firmly as a complement rather than a competitor to the church. The primary source of enthusiasm and leadership for renewal developed on the Notre Dame campus among the younger members of the Department of Religion and in the community at large. By the end of 1971 the movement had expanded to include annual conventions, regional meetings, newsletters, and considerable one-to-one evangelism among those as yet unbaptized by the Spirit.[18]

As in the early days of the Jesus movement in California, the mass media gave the Catholic Pentecostal phenomenon considerable attention. Already a doctoral dissertation has been written on the subject, with special concentration on perhaps the most representative community in the renewal, that of Ann Arbor, Michigan.[19] It was given the name "The Word of God" community. Starting soon after the Duquesne meeting in 1967 as a weekly prayer meeting, The Word quickly grew in number to include by February, 1972, some two hundred fifty members, with another one hundred fifty in preparation for membership. Some 70 percent are students; the rest are townspeople, with strong representation from the university. A surprisingly low 65 percent are Roman Catholic, suggesting that this movement at least is extending into the larger community. A series of four subcommittees administer the details of applications, standards, and physical needs.

As the movement grew out to include full-time communal residences, much like the Jesus houses (although with no drug rehabilitation involved), it made several crucial decisions: it does not own property; and it organizes itself around the concept of "households"—special groups for prayer, for healing, for celibates, and for married people. All meals are shared in common; group study is expected of all; and the household chores are divided equally. In each household the members are required to work closely with fellow members in determining the steps they will follow in joint growth in the life of the Holy Spirit.[20]

What struck some observers was that a strong, genuine expression of love and joy and enthusiasm seemed to prevail throughout the community. Despite inevitable personal differences, the members seem to be growing in religious maturity and insight in their new communal life. They are sure they have found the secret to continued renewal in Christian life and thus find themselves relatively free from doubts and fears. They avoid any heavy theologizing about charisms but state that their community rests on four assumptions, which they buttress with biblical proof texts. First, God loves every person and has a personal plan for everyone's life. Second, man's sinful nature has prevented man from taking advantage of God's love; however, man still has free will and can choose evil. Third, only through Jesus Christ can man hope to find fulfillment in God's love. Finally, to learn of God's plan which liberates him from sin, each person must accept Christ as his Lord and Savior; this must be done through faith and prayer.[21]

The members are eager to explain the transforming power of the baptism by the Spirit to others. They know from personal experience that their faith in Christ has led him to work miracles in their lives. Believers find financial resources which they had not received before their conversion. Some have found release from physical ills after receiving the Spirit. In this they learned, however, that the University hospital did not take kindly to their praying at the bedside of a sick brother long after visiting hours. Some of these practices have also left something of a strain between the community and the Roman Catholic clergy of Ann Arbor.[22]

Evaluations of the Word of God group have been made by several who were once members but have resigned. Some objected to the traditional role of women, who do little but "stay home and have babies" while the men evangelize. Others believe the community was too introspective, caught up in its own world and giving little attention to outside interests. Some thought it was too close to Roman Catholicism; others feared it had moved too far away.

What does seem true about the Ann Arbor Jesus people is that many members have found in communal living answers to religious needs which had not been met before. Communal life at Ann Arbor provides warmth and acceptance and the promise of virtually unlimited spiritual growth in the use of the charisms; at the same time it has none of the enforced discipline of those denominations having just one liturgy, one creed, and one interpretation of the Bible. The observers believe that if this kind of new-time religion is going to succeed at all, it will trace its beginning to Ann Arbor.[23] Like the Jesus kids, the Catholic Pentecostals believe they are following Jesus all the way. The fact that every newly organized form of religious community has started with the same kind of enthusiasm only to turn finally to more formal structures of expression, does not deter this community from believing that through the renewal of the gifts it has found the means by which faith can be kept open and spontaneous and growing.

7

THE PERIMETER
OF REVIVAL:
COMMUNES
AND FRINGE
GROUPS

The new-time religion is leading some of its converts to explore the implications of St. Paul's words, "When anyone is united to Christ, there is a new world; the older order has gone, and a new order has already begun." Convinced that by their new birth they are living in this world, several small but highly dedicated groups of Christians are creating new social expressions of their faith. Today's revival inspires them to live out their newness in rural communes, or fulltime "communities of commitment," all of which are on the perimeter of traditional church life in America. An examination of these communities as they emerged in the late 1960s provides further evidence of the uniqueness of today's revival in contrast to those of the past.

Rural Communes

While most of the Jesus houses are located in large urban areas to facilitate the work of drug rehabilitation and to train for street witnessing, some of the Jesus people are returning to the isolation of rural life. This migration closely parallels that of the secular counter culture, responsible for hundreds of rural communes that have sprung up since about 1968.[1] In several respects the Christian rural communes and the secular counterparts resemble one another. They both acknowledge their reliance for inspiration and guidance on earlier collectivist programs such as the Koinonia Farm in Georgia, the Catholic Worker Farm, and the Bruderhof Community in New York.[2] While these organizations by choice have maintained direct business relations with the outside world, the Christian and secular communes seek to go beyond such dependence. They have committed themselves to building true communities independent of the straight world.

Both kinds of rural communes are seeking "liberation" from domination by material things—automobiles, mortgages, insurance, television. Once liberated, they believe they can pursue a more authentic life style. This is achieved, they believe, when man restores his proper relationship with the land. By returning to simple farming, the believer links himself to the life cycle expressed in the seasons: birth, growth, fulfillment, death, and rebirth.

By blending in with nature rather than dominating it, the believer regains that ancestral wisdom known to the true communities of the past. He learns joy and peace by serving the creation rather than serving himself. Beyond that, secular and Christian rural communalists know they can accomplish this restoration only by living in community rather than in isolation. In community living they find that they draw strength and love from each other and are able to make a clean and permanent break with the past.[3] At one commune, Drop City, the group celebrates this new life:

> We are alive. We dance the Joy-dance. We listen to the eternal rhythm. Our feet move to unity, a balanced step of beauty and strength. Creation is joy. Joy is love. Life, love, joy, energy are one. We are all one. Can you hear the music? Come dance with us.[4]

Not all of the rural communes are Christian, but at least a few are trying to absorb the new-time religion into their lives by blending Christian teachings with those of other world religions. Among the best known of those with an eclectic approach are the several communes clustered in Taos County, New Mexico. Located there are Lorien with some 30 members, New Buffalo with the same number, Lama Foundation with 25, and Morningstar with more than 50. Other comparable experiments are at Drop City in southern Colorado, at Sunny Valley, the Family of the Mystic Arts, in Oregon. Similar but less widely known groups are found in at least 34 states. One student of the movement thinks several hundred others have started but soon failed.[5]

Those rural communities dedicated to an explicit Christian life share several characteristics. Many of the members are former alcoholics or drug addicts, or people who have deserted or were deserted by their spouses or families; some are runaway teen-agers. Rather than try to return to straight society through the traditional means of rehabilitation, they have made a complete break with that society. They hope that step will restore the inner resources they need to survive in a hostile world. Since the communes keep no records or statistics, there is no way of knowing how many participants who are rehabilitated return to the regular society and how many remain at the commune. Apparently some of the cured go on to start new communes.

Something of the wide variation of methods used to carry out these programs is seen by an examination of two specific communities—Living Waters in Oregon and the Children of God, which has communes in several states.

Living Waters was founded by a former professional wrestler known only as Bill. By early 1971 it consisted of some 20 members, mostly young adults. By choice it isolates itself from any formal denominational ties. Some years ago, as a joke, Bill had attended a revivalist meeting of a faith healer. At the altar call, his friends pushed him forward. But at the moment the preacher laid on his hands, Bill started to speak in tongues. Shortly after that the wrestler brought his son, born with a club foot, to the revival meeting. At the moment of baptism, the boy started to walk without a visible limp. That convinced Bill he must start his life over again as a Christian. On the advice of his minister, he and his family opened Living Waters as a rural commune. From its beginning the program ministered primarily to drug users who could not find help in the urban community. The close family style living plus the direct identification with the cleansing power of the land are the ingredients used for rehabilitation.[6]

Bill explained his faith to a reporter: "The Spirit will put you in tune with God. It is His language. People who speak it can be healed of both the ills of the body and the sickness of the mind." Those who have received the gift of tongues and healing—as Bill stated it, who "bear Christ's witness that he is meant to stay here"— are accepted as full members of the commune. Apparently, those without these gifts receive no invitation to remain.[7]

As is true of other Pentecostals, Living Waters residents use their special gift as a source of group identity. They keep alive this uniqueness by their daily "sharing session." Each member shares what he thinks is important at that particular moment; this could be an incident from his past, a dream, a new feeling of love, or whatever strikes him at the time. During these sessions speaking in tongues is also used to help cure some of the smaller illnesses of the members, such as rashes or infections. Apparently, as one reporter found after visiting there, the program at Living Waters has helped at least some of the members rid themselves of their addiction.[8]

Although detailed information on similar communities is hard to uncover, several programs following Bill's plan are conducted in other areas. Christian communes are in operation at Antioch Farm near Mendocino, California; at the several Shiloh Houses in Oregon; at Emmanuel Farm near Sumas, Washington; at Love Inn near Freeville, New York; and at Love Valley in rural North Carolina. Many participants insist on total anonymity largely because they are attempting rehabilitation and want no publicity from inquiring reporters or public health officers. Any public notice could well destroy or seriously weaken such programs, especially those with little experience.[9]

The Children of God: A Commune That Failed

It is a long way from the calm and sheltering farm at Living Waters to the regimented and aggressive communes of the Children of God. Yet, with its several ranches scattered throughout the nation, this movement also represents the impact of the new-time religion on a wide variety of individuals who are suddenly brought together in the hope of a new life. Easily the most controversial, not to say fanatic, and to many the most unpopular of all the Jesus people groups is the Children of God. By the end of 1971 the membership embraced from 2,000 to 3,000 persons, mostly teen-agers and young adults. But at the moment of its greatest numerical strength, it started coming apart.

In one sense the Children of God belong more to the urban Jesus movement than the rural commune scene since some of its headquarters and much of its witness are in Los Angeles and other large cities. At the same time, much of its activity is centered on several ranches, deliberately isolated from the straight world. Whatever the label, the Children of God are like no other group.

Until recently, the historical origins of the movement were heavily clouded over by rumor, gossip, and hearsay. Three members of Westmont College, California, however, made a detailed study of the background and their findings help considerably in trying to sort out the workings of the Children.[10]

David Berg and Fred Jordan, both licensed pastors,

were the two men most responsible for launching the movement. Berg, with a family of four children, started working for Jordan, a radio evangelist in Los Angeles. Berg's responsibility was to help promote Jordan's program and to find new stations for this ministry. Apparently the two could not settle a dispute over whether one of Berg's sons should continue to live on Jordan's ranch in Texas, and they parted ways.

Around the end of 1967 Berg became involved in a coffee house for teen-agers in Huntington Beach and quickly won over several converts to his preaching. These joined the Berg family in creating a commune directed by Berg. The program at the house was much like that of the House of Acts in trying to rehabilitate addicts through religious conversion. Berg and the group then started touring the West coast, adding a few converts here and there but without any fixed base of operations. It was at this point that members of the group started calling themselves the "Children of God," comparing their plight to the wandering Jews in the desert searching for the promised land. They apparently believed they were the contemporary chosen people of God who alone could understand the will of the Almighty for his favored people. They gave themselves Old Testament names; they patterned their economic life after the *kibbutzim* of Israel; and they started dressing as they believed the Jews dressed in the desert.

On occasion, dressed in sack cloth garb, the Children would attend a church service. They would shout "Woe" or "Repent," and were usually asked to leave. They welcomed this since it reinforced in their minds how far from God's will the established churches had moved. These events had a more important result, however. They attracted public attention and some television coverage in the greater Los Angeles area. For the first time the general public learned about the Children of God.

That exposure led Jordan to make peace with Berg and the group. He allowed them to live at his ranch where they made substantial physical improvements. At the ranch the first formal structure of communal living appeared under Berg's direction of the 100 to 150 residents. Everyone joined a tribe, each named after one of the twelve of the Old Testament, and surrendered himself to the full authority of the leader. Each tribe had some special economic function for the good of the whole community, such as farming, livestock, or carpentry. Some worked in crafts to sell to the outside world.

Jordan then saw the opportunities to use the children to promote his new television program, "Church in the Home." He gave the group full access to his warehouse in a rundown part of Los Angeles. This quickly became the national headquarters for the group. Under the direction of Berg's son Arnold ("Joshua") Dietrich, the program started a vigorous campaign of recruiting street people in the city, and within a short time young people started joining. They learned more about the Children from the television exposure given by Jordan in which apparently the more fanatic and eccentric teachings and practices of the group were camouflaged as Jordan told his audiences about this new band which was carrying out God's will among the delinquents of the area.[11] For those teen-agers not attracted to the other Jesus movement programs, but who were looking for some kind of communal or family shelter, the Children of God proved irresistible.

They started enlisting first one by one, then by the dozens.

However, just as it seemed that some sort of stability would be achieved for the program, in September, 1971, Jordan found himself forced to drive the Children off his property. By then he had also given them use of a ranch of his near Coachella, California. When he learned the leader there was not using the property as he had ordered, he tried to have that leader removed. Such interference in the life of the community could not be tolerated by the Children. They insisted on keeping their appointed leader at the ranch, and the entire community then walked out. From that point on, without any further use of any of Jordan's property, they have divided into several dozen small and largely autonomous bands, living throughout the United States; a few also have taken up the cause in western Europe.[12]

To add to their problems, the Children found that the parents of several members were forming a Parents' Committee to Save our Sons and Daughters from the Children of God Organization. They charged that the group had virtually kidnapped their children against their wills, had used brainwashing and hypnotic techniques to keep the children in a commune, and had taught them to hate their parents.

These charges, all denied by the leaders of the movement, are best understood by examining in some detail the teachings and practices of the Children. The religious doctrines are those common to many teen-age Jesus revival groups, but in the Children of God movement they are enforced with far greater intensity. Every moment of every day is carefully planned to inculcate into the members the truth of the teachings they study. The foundation is the Bible, but the method is memorization of as many verses as possible without any serious attempt at interpretation. Indeed, the elders tell the Children that any deviation from their teachings is the work of the devil and must be resisted at all costs. Much of the day's routine is spent in solitary and group memorization of specified texts.

The Children also hold to a rigid apocalyptic premillennial interpretation of the end of the world. They have no doubts that the last days are now here, and they point to the wars, earthquakes, and decline of public morals as their proof. Therefore they believe they must separate themselves from the rest of the world to remain pure and prepared for the imminent second coming of Jesus. Since the planet is soon to be destroyed, one has no need to study in college or hold a permanent job or in any way become involved in the corrupt outside world. Those diversions are only tricks played by Satan to lure the Children away from their true calling of total obedience.

Finally, among their teachings is a heavy accent on the Pentecostal experience of baptism by the Holy Spirit. Despite long hours of prayer, sacrifice of personal comforts, loss of the security of family and home, the Child of God learns he receives a far greater reward, the coming of the gifts of healing and tongues and prophecy and whatever else the Spirit wishes to bestow on him for the preservation of the community.

Every part of the daily routine and the practices of the Children reinforces their separateness. Where the lives of members once were disorganized, undisciplined, and self-centered, now the regimen is one of unquestioned obedience to the recognized authorities who speak with the power of God. Everyone rises at the same time, 6:45 a.m., and engages for several hours in Bible memorization, group leadership training, and household chores. Then at 11:00 a.m. they eat the first meal of the day, followed by more classes, more work on special tribal assignments, and more memorization. After the evening meal, the program consists mostly of services of inspiration and praise, all intended to consolidate group feeling.

Those who pass this period of training begin a second phase, intended to provide street witnesses for recruiting. Most of the indoctrination is on-the-job training with the Children spending considerable time on busy street corners in Los Angeles or wherever their tribe is located. In contrast to many of the other Jesus people groups, the Children do not attempt to discuss issues or Bible verses with passersby. They shout a verse or two, or hand out a tract, and move on to the next person. They are sure they have the answers to the great questions and find no need to do more than announce this to outsiders.

Once a member has been through the indoctrination and witnessing phases of his training, he takes to the highways with his tribe to add more recruits and to deliver the witness. The adding of new recruits is essential for the economic life of each tribe. Much of the money used by the elders is given them by a new recruit. When he is accepted into the Children, he is required without exception to turn over all his property and whatever cash he has. In this manner he is taught the blessings of following the first Christians after Pentecost, who shared all things in common.[13] He learns also his complete dependence on the group for his life in this world and the next. He has committed himself to the cause, which has ended his questioning and self-centeredness; what is left now is to wait for Jesus.

These economic arrangements have produced considerable criticism from many, not the least from parents who were upset not only over the absence of their child but over the bank accounts, automobiles, musical instruments, clothing and personal effects the young person gave up.[14] However, other observers noted that this asceticism has not weakened the zealous loyalty of the convert to the group. A student reporter for the University of Texas *Daily Texan* visited the ranch there and reported: "It is hard to imagine so many people happy, so full of joy with so few material possessions. The harmony and fellowship between each member cannot be realized except by direct observation. Peaceful expressions grace the members' faces and eyes. One immediately is touched by their sincere expressions of concern. . . . One can see why they live a fantastic life, filled with love, companionship, concern, and service to others." [15] The Westmont College faculty reported much the same enthusiasm, noting that the Children seemed healthy and well-fed and sincerely interested in their visitors. They were served ice cream and cake, and then treated to an evening of song and worship. The members also joined in with the rock combo, and after singing came spirited dancing of Hebrew folk dances.[16]

By mid-1972, however, such moments of bliss could not bring back the heyday of tribal community known only two years before. The split between Jordan and the tribes could not be healed; the unfavorable national publicity created by the parents' group could not be undone. Finally, the tribes seem to divide into smaller and smaller units to disperse across the country, not out of loyalty to a greater mission, but because of internal disputes which have not become public.

Two such tangles did come to light when the Children recruited the most influential leader of teen-age Jesus people in Atlanta, David Hoyt, and in Seattle, Linda Meissner. Both Hoyt and Meissner expected their own followers to join them in the move. When this failed to happen, both the original groups and the Children were divided badly over the split. These divisions have shown no signs of mending.[17] What might have become a model rural Christian commune fell victim to the human frailties of suspicion, resentment, and jealousy; the experience of the Children shows the difficulty of the participants in learning to live together.

Three on the Fringe

In this day of innovation in religious life, it is not surprising that several spokesmen would come forward claiming to have discovered the first pure and correct interpretation of the Word since Pentecost. Such is the inspiration in the 1970s for several groups which have grown quickly in recent years. Their leaders all point out that it is "time to get back to the fundamentals"; or it is "time to purify the churches" in an age gone crazy with experiments and fads. Each spokesman puts forward his program as the return to the fundamentals as the pure church.

Three such groups present their own strategy for returning to basic Christianity, but each also reflects the impact of the new-time religion on its program. Whatever the soundness of their claims to authenticity, they are supported by people who want to express their faith and who find one of these fringe groups more congenial to their needs than the established churches.

The Way

Among the better publicized groups is The Way Biblical Research Center of New Knoxville, Ohio. Founded in the 1950s by the Reverend Victor Paul Wierwille, it attracted no national attention until after the editors at *Life* and *Time* linked it to the growing Jesus revival. Wierwille stated at that time that The Way already had at least ten thousand members living in all parts of the country. He said he avoided a headcount because he did not want to dilute the religious witness by overemphasizing statistics. However, Wierwille pointed to the connection with the Jesus movement by showing that two of his important leaders were original members in the House of Acts commune in San Francisco in 1967, Steve Heefner and Jim Doop.[18]

The Way defies any precise label. Basing its teachings exclusively on his interpretations of the Bible, Wierwille claims that his is the only true biblical program today. He draws on both his academic training at Chicago Divinity School and Princeton Theological Seminary, and on a quarter century's personal research to present a unique reevaluation of traditional Protestant doctrine. He teaches that every word in the Bible is equally and infallibly true, but that different books of the Bible are intended for certain groups of believers. For instance, the Old Testament was the Scripture for the Jewish people, the four Gospels are for "gentiles," and the rest of the New Testament is for the "Church of God," consisting of "born-again believers." He gives most of his attention to the letters of St. Paul, with special focus on Ephesians, which he believes summarizes all of Christian teaching.

Wierwille is willing to relegate the four Gospels to mere "gentiles" because he rejects the Christian doctrine of the Trinity. To him the teaching smacks of paganism. He insists that Jesus is truly the Son of God, but is not coequal with God. To him the doctrine of the Incarnation is only an admission by Christians that they do not really understand the true place of Jesus' relationship to God. Similarly the idea that the Holy Spirit is coequal with the other two persons of the Trinity makes no sense to Wierwille. God is continually present in the world, so Christianity needs no third person to explain that presence.[19]

The program of The Way, however, extends far beyond theological reformulation. In its introductory brochure, a spokesman claims it has "helped thousands of people in many different ways. People full of fear and worry have become people with great confidence and believing. People with marital problems have overcome them and developed a strong and joyful marriage relationship. People without meaning to their lives have received great meaning and purpose." The same help has been received by persons ineffective in their prayer lives, and those with health problems "have seen and manifested God's healing power;" drug addicts have also been cured.[20]

Wierwille says these achievements are the results of small-group study of the Bible. He offers a program of study which provides "a maximum of information in a minimum of time," taking in "all of the basic key concepts" of the Bible to create the abundant life. The requirements for anyone wanting to start with the "foundational biblical research class" is as follows: pre-registration with the promise to attend every class session; a payment of $65; the use of the King James Version of the Bible; withholding of questions by the enrollee until the final question-and-answer session; abstention from taking personal notes during a class and reliance instead on a syllabus and study guide furnished by The Way; completion of take-home assignments for each class period; and agreeing to read all assigned materials for the course. For those not able to come to New Knoxville, The Way furnishes the name of the nearest chapter.

From this foundational course, more detailed studies are offered with the same format. These deal in more depth with the issues raised in the first course. Frequent regional rallies are held to promote new memberships, and the heaviest emphasis in advertising is to those under thirty. A basic staple in the ministry is the summer family camp in which the members are able to share their experience with fellow believers. Wierwille himself exudes a "mod" image, with flashy cowboy suits and a large Harley-Davidson motorcycle.

In one important respect, the Wierwille program is related to several Jesus revival groups; there is a heavy emphasis on speaking in tongues. But Wierwille tells converts in the movement to open their mouths "and let out any sounds that come." To him speaking in tongues is not the direct result of the Baptism of the Holy Spirit but can be learned; one has only to work at it.[21]

The Way helps inquirers by offering a large supply of

films, film strips, and tapes with messages by the leader on issues such as Oriental religions. Members can also purchase rings, tie tacs, cuff links, pendants, and earrings in the form of the Dove of Peace. No item costs over $97.50. For those wishing to hear the study tapes on their own equipment, The Way offers a three speed reel recorder for $100.[22]

With a multi-media teaching program aimed at solving the member's personal problems, The Way continues to grow. It carefully avoids the divisive issue of contemporary politics or direct competition with established churches. It follows earlier revival teachings in its emphasis on the Bible and on the need for individual conversion. But its rewriting of the doctrine of the Trinity and its abstention from involving itself in the daily work of the churches suggests again how new today's revival in America is.

The Process Church

Farther out on the fringe of experimental groups is the more urban Process Church of the Final Judgment which appeared in the late 1960s. The primary source of information about the group is found in its brochure, "So Be It," distributed by members in New York, Chicago, and Boston at busy street corners. Usually the members wear a distinctive uniform for their street witnessing. It consists of a vaguely ecclesiastical suit and cape with the coat collars decorated with red three-horned goat heads. Below those horns is a large silver cross; at other times similar esoteric symbols are added. The brochure claims that these signs all point to the wisdom of The Process Church; its purpose is to embrace the full truth of all religions. The key doctrine is a kind of "trinity" of equal gods, which is the fountain of knowledge; these are Jehovah, Lucifer, and Satan. Jesus comes into the picture as a supernatural being with unifying powers to reconcile the contradictory demands of the three gods of the trinity. Each member expresses this sense of unity in his formal garb, consisting of three colors: black to show the reality of death, red as a reminder of the blood shed for all men, and white to represent the light of new life in The Process Church.

While the formal doctrine does not go much beyond that, the members have worked out a carefully detailed daily schedule. Almost all of the estimated 500 members in the United States live in communal houses in the largest cities. They keep their communes immaculately clean and given equal attention to their personal appearance, since they do not want to be classified as hippies. They provide their own livelihood by producing crafts such as earrings, beads, necklaces, and rings. They also solicit donations, and some operate coffee shops open to the public.

The real strength in the movement apparently is in the sense of solidarity created by their small group sessions. For both beginners and advanced members, these programs center on discussions of personal problems with an attempt to purge guilt feelings through group confession. The members practice Esalen-type sensitivity sessions, such as "trust walks" or being blindfolded and touching another's face. At one session, Peter Rowley participated with the new members in chanting deliberately meaningless phrases, such as "Dadum . . . Ladadeda . . . Dum . . . Dalada." Then all joined in readings by members on

Lucifer, Christ, Jehovah, and Satan. This was followed by a discussion on Fire, Earth, Air, and Water. Then, Rowley relates, "We shouted the names of Satan, Lucifer, Jehovah and Christ. After each one we clapped our hands. At one stage there was organized but wild shouting, the beating of a drum, and "Sister Julia," a sweet, shy girl, urged me to shake a *mariachi,* which I did." [23]

Members of The Process Church seem to come from broken homes, drug or alcoholism backgrounds, or from radical political groups. Like the eclectic rural communes of New Mexico, the Process groups are searching for the one final religious system which they believe will restore peace and brotherhood.

The Followers of Jesus

A third organization, also on the outer fringe of today's revival, is a group which insists on keeping its true title anonymous, but is called by one of its more careful students, "Followers of Jesus." [24] The desire for secrecy suggests that its members do not believe they can effectively change or reform the direction of American life, but can prepare themselves for the life hereafter.

Located originally in Tulsa, Oklahoma, and consisting of some six hundred members in several cities, the Followers resemble the Process in several ways. Most are young adults from the drug, alcohol, or political scene. Most are college educated, and all prefer to live in communes. None has found the established churches to be compatible with their religious needs.

The unique feature of this group is that it attempts to remain as close as possible to the Roman Catholic Church without really being Catholic. The members uphold the same system of sacraments, changing only the teaching on confirmation. They acknowledge that a pope exists but they reject his authority over their lives. They consider themselves to be members of a religious order similar to those of the Catholic Church. The members live in small, virtually monastic settings, carefully avoiding sexual relations or use of any stimulants. They provide for themselves by taking on general housework, painting, and lawn maintenance.

Every day they celebrate communion at the same time as fellow members across the nation—6:15 p.m. They maintain close contact with the several houses, but each remains financially and ecclesiastically independent. They all follow the same procedure in admitting new members. These are mostly young adults, who first become novitiates; then after study and work they are considered by the elders to be eligible for taking "eternal vows." Those who accept the vows are made priests. No distinction is made between men and women in terms of authority.

Like The Way, The Followers believe they are loyal to the original teachings of the church. They are convinced they have returned to the true fundamentals of the faith and have preserved the purity of that faith. One priest told Rowley, "We are in the Apostolic Succession. Basically we are Early Christians. We are the Church before the Eastern rite split from Rome." [25]

8

THAT NEW-TIME RELIGION

With unexpected speed and in widely varying forms the Jesus revival has established itself on the American religious scene. In this summary I will show why this outpouring is a "new-time religion" compared to earlier revivals. I will try to show why the principal groups studied in this book constitute the core of the Jesus movement, while other organizations which seem close to it really are separate and parallel. I hope, further, to show why many of the common criticisms of the Jesus revival are themselves open to criticism. Finally, I would like to suggest what the immediate future for that new-time religion in America is, and what the organized churches and concerned individuals can do to help everyone involved in the movement.

A New-time Revival

Without qualification it can be said the new-time religion is indeed a revival—a sudden, spontaneous expression of commitment to the Christian faith through the process of instant conversion. Further, this movement shares several features in common with the earlier great revivals. Its understanding of Christian teaching is evangelical rather than analytic; its source of authority is the Bible as the verbally inspired, inerrant word of God; it believes in the efficacy of instant conversion; and it emerged during a time of grave national crisis. All of these elements were also found in the revivals of Moody, Sunday, and Graham.

Yet much of the general misunderstanding today concerning the Jesus revival comes from the fact that many observers think it is one more traditional revival. Such a conclusion does not stand up under a careful examination of those important features of the new-time religion which are markedly different from earlier revivals. The Jesus people carefully avoid the organized, mass-scale, celebrity-led revivals started by Moody and carried on by Sunday and Graham. The Jesus people cherish small groups and decentralized religious witnessing programs. They enthusiastically cultivate a spontaneous openness to innovation, change and experimentation. While this sometimes leads to aimless rap sessions or demoralized leaderless communal houses, to the new converts the risk is worth taking. Exceptions to this avoidance of large groups would be the Inter-Varsity Christian Fellowship, which has a national mass rally every three years, and Campus Crusade, which sponsors six to eight large scale regional rallies annually.

The heart of their work, however, is done on a one-to-one basis on the campus or in other areas of witnessing.

One reason contributing to the great popularity of earlier revivalist leaders, as William G. McLoughlin suggested, was that they rekindled the enthusiasm for the American dream by loyalty to traditional political and religious values. Today's Jesus revivalists, in the teen-age, college, and adult groupings, show a marked indifference to any signs of patriotic demonstration. Some, such as the Christian World Liberation Front, have been active in the anti-war movement; in no commune or related Jesus movement program can visible signs of the traditional red-white-and-blue nationalism of a Moody, Sunday, or Graham be found.

Another important American institution which earlier revivalists upheld devoutly was belief in the sanctity of private property. The great revival preachers never seriously challenged the American love affair with laissez faire free enterprise, the moral rights of ownership of property over those of organized labor, or the right of an individual to enjoy all the material rewards of his economic initiative. On every level of today's new-time religion we find a massive indifference, and often a marked hostility, towards these older attitudes. Communal living is practiced by many of the teen-age and rural Jesus people, and in the Catholic Pentecostal communities. The participants believe they are following the dictates of the New Testament in living collectively. Beyond that, among those who hold to a firm apocalyptic premillennialism, there is a firm conviction that the Christian is wasting time when he gives sustained attention to income or property or related financial matters. He must instead be witnessing for the Lord because the end of the world draws near.

Furthermore, the college evangelicals—but not the teen-agers or rural communalists—show a far deeper concern with such complex and massive contemporary problems as war, racism, pollution, and poverty than did earlier evangelicals. The students believe their conversion leads them to adopt a totally new way of serving God, and the outlet they find for this appears in much stronger social commitment than their predecessors. However, it must be added that the teen-agers and rural participants for the most part show little interest in such issues. They are more involved in individual renewal and growth after their second birth.

With some exceptions, most of today's Jesus people show a marked suspicion or indifference to working within the framework of established churches. Many times because of their counter-culture hairdos, clothes, and spontaneous behavior they have been ignored or rebuffed by the churches. By comparison to the converts from the earlier great revivals of Moody and the others, today's new believers rarely want to join a traditional congregation. If necessary, they start their own congregations, or maintain their own group identity where they are participating with established parish programs.

It is at this point apparently that many who feel today's revival is an old-time outpouring make a serious misjudgment. They believe the new converts should come to them and ask what they can do to help the churches. With but few exceptions, this is not taking place.

Unity and Diversity

On balance, the differences between the old- and new-time revivals heavily outweigh the similarities. This does not mean that today's outpouring is a unified protest against the less desirable traits of earlier revivalism. Significant differences in organization, theology, and behavior do exist among today's Jesus people. Some groups enforce rules prohibiting smoking, card playing, modern dancing, or watching television, playing records or the radio. Some prohibit the use of any books or other reading materials other than the Bible and related biblical aids. For others, however, these are not important issues, and each individual is allowed to make his own decisions so long as his preferences do not interfere with the growth of a brother or sister in their community. Some Jesus movements, such as the Children of God, are closed societies where no deviation exists as to daily schedule, religious beliefs, or behavior. Others such as Calvary Chapel of Costa Mesa, carefully avoid regimentation and instead offer a varied program of meetings, concerts, and discussions. The Catholic Pentecostals want to remain Roman Catholic, yet be free to explore their new life in the Holy Spirit; thus many of their doctrines stand in marked contrast with the more simple Protestantism of, say, a rural commune in Oregon.

For all this diversity, substantial cohesion and unity does exist among those caught up in the new revival. Three themes or goals stand out as the principal characteristics of today's Jesus people. First, they all show a total dedication to the teachings, ministry, and redemptive life of Jesus. They find in him the authority, direction, and love

123

they consider totally adequate for their lives. They know of no other person, institution, doctrine, or body of wisdom which so completely commands their full loyalty.

Secondly, unity among Jesus followers emerges out of their willingness to make a clean break with their former habits and values. This leads the teen-age drug user to break his habit and turn to full-time evangelism; it leads the college evangelical to break with his tradition—perhaps even that of his parents—and to work out the social implications of the gospel; and it leads the rural communalist to give up his job, friends, life style, and position in his community. Among all three groups this sense of disciplined dedication is decisive. By definition, this excludes a large number of teen-agers and young adults who are involved with some parts of the Jesus revival such as Bible raps, ocean baptisms, and rock concerts, but who continue to live with their family and thus remain in the same educational and socio-economic class. It is from this group that much of the membership for denominational youth programs is drawn, movements which are parallel to, but separate from new-time revivalism.

Thirdly, the Jesus revolution is united by the joyous enthusiasm of its participants for living, worshipping, and growing together, especially with one's own age group. They are dedicated to sharing their new life in such forms as communes, group witnessing, and group Bible study. They respect the individuality of each brother and sister, while also seeking to draw out the best qualities of each one to strengthen the unity of the group.

Thus, in my judgment, the teen-age drug culture dropouts, the evangelical students and Pentecostals, and the rural communalists share these three common goals;

dedication to the new life in Jesus, a willingness to change one's entire life style, and a recognition of the communal character of the Christian life. Exception to these goals can be found; qualifications are always in order. Sometimes the lines separating the original Jesus people from the parallel groups are blurred.

Critics of the Jesus People

The variety of groups and the accent on feeling over analysis has come under considerable criticism by observers of the movement. Some church spokesmen point out with ample documentation that in some Jesus groups little effort is made to lead the new converts into understanding the more substantial and challenging dimensions of the Christian faith. In some houses the members are given specific Bible verses to memorize with little further attention given to studying the unity and complexity of the Scriptures. Some critics hold up the highly zealous Children of God as representative of almost all Jesus people groups. Observers from the political left find the language of old-fashioned revivalism used by the Jesus kids to be proof the youngsters are being manipulated by the capitalist establishment to accept religion as an opiate to drug them against joining in the struggle for liberation of the oppressed. Some close students of the movement object to the lack of theological sophistication by the leaders, or to the emotional pitch of some group meetings.

What Will the Future Be?

What these criticisms and observations suggest is that the Jesus movement now faces a broader task than at its beginning. Not only do its participants have to convert and minister to street people, but they must find ways to direct and sustain their own joy and enthusiasm of the older convert and continue to grow in the Christian faith. This cannot be done by ignoring the resources built up over nineteen hundred years of Christianity. Somehow both the established churches and the Jesus people who are sincerely looking for continued growth must find a way to sustain and enrich each other. This kind of rapport has taken place, such as is seen in the program of Hollywood Presbyterian Church, led by Don Williams as related in his book *Call to the Streets*. With a PhD from Columbia University and Union Theological Seminary, Williams, a pastor of an established congregation, has demonstrated the opportunities which are available to others who make the effort.

The attempt at reconciliation must come also from the churches if they want to keep alive in a day when membership, attendance, and stewardship are all in decline. Several tangible steps are available to all churches, even though many may not have any Jesus people in or near their community. They can make new efforts at strengthening family relationships as the most effective means of reducing the number of teen-agers joining the drug culture. Secondly, the churches can increase their support for those experimental ministries which are attempting to work with the dropouts and street people. Finally, the churches can be better prepared to live with the new generation when they recognize the Jesus movement is not out to destroy the existing structures, nor put pipe organs and Bach on the shelf in favor of guitars and rock and roll. The churches can accept the criticisms made of them by the Jesus people as the first steps needed to be taken to bridge the gulf which so often today divides them.

The Jesus people are saying to the organized churches they are not impressed with the elaborate programs, the cautious approaches to experimental ministries, and the ecclesiastical bureaucracies. They call instead for freshness, spontaneity, and enthusiasm. These are not comfortable nor predictable themes with which to live. But then neither is the promise of Jesus to make all things new.

NOTES

Introduction

1. Coleman, "The Coming World Revival?", *Christianity Today,* July 16, 1971, p. 958

2. See his speech, "Jesus Christ, Lord of All: A Challenge to America's Evangelists," *United Evangelical Action,* Summer, 1971, pp. 13, 40.

3. Duane Pederson, *Jesus People* (Pasadena: Compass Books, 1971), pp. 120, 122, 128

4. See Willmar Thorkelson, "This Week in Religion," *Minneapolis Star,* September 25, 1971, p. 13A.

Chapter 1

1. McLoughlin, Billy Graham: *Revivalist in a Secular Age* (New York: Ronald Press, 1960), pp. 19, 24

2. Alan Heimart and Perry Miller, eds., *The Great Awaken-*

ing (Indianapolis: The Bobbs-Merrill Company, 1967), pp. xiv-lxi.

3. Barton W. Stone, as quoted in L. W. Bacon, *A History of American Christianity* (New York: Scribner, 1900), p. 234.

4. William G. McLoughlin Jr., *Modern Revivalism: Charles Grandison Finney to Billy Graham* (New York: Ronald press, 1959), p. 16

5. p. 105.

6. James F. Findlay Jr., *Dwight L. Moody, American Evangelist, 1837–1899* (Chicago: University of Chicago Press, 1969), pp. 274-83; McLoughlin, *Modern Revivalism,* chapter 5; Grover C. Loud, *Evangelized America* (New York: Dial Press, 1928), chapter 16

7. McLoughlin, *Modern Revivalism,* p. 435

8. p. 446

Chapter 2

1. Graham, *Calling Youth to Christ* (Grand Rapids: Zondervan, 1947), p. 29

2. Graham, *Revival in Our Time* (Wheaton: Van Kampen Press, 1950), pp. 71-75; *America's Hour of Decision* (Wheaton: Van Kampen Press, 1951), p. 119

3. Graham, *Hour of Decision,* pp. 144, 141

4. p. 119

5. Curtis Mitchell, *God in the Garden* (Garden City, N.Y.: Doubleday and Co., 1957), *passim;* George M. Wilson, ed., *Twenty Years Under God: Proclaiming the Gospel of Jesus Christ to the World* (Minneapolis: World Wide Publications, 1971), p. 140

6. "Men Must Be Changed Before a Nation Can," *Life,* June 6, 1960. Copyright 1972 Time Inc.

Chapter 3

1. Ahlstrom, "The Moral and Theological Revolution of the 1960s and Its Implications for American Religious History," Herbert J. Bass, ed., *The State of American History* (New York: Quadrangle Books, 1970), pp. 103, 100

2. George Gallup Jr., and John O. Davis, eds., *Religion in America, 1971,* The Gallup Opinion Index, April, 1971, Report No. 70, p. 48

3. pp. 43-50, 68-91

Chapter 4

1. Novak, *A Theology for Radical Politics* (New York: Herder and Herder, 1969), pp. 21-22

2. For a full discussion, see Robert L. Johnson, *Counter Culture and the Vision of God* (Minneapolis: Augsburg Publishing House, 1971)

3. *Ibid.*, 106-18; Theodore Roszak, *The Making of a Counter Culture* (New York: Doubleday Anchor Books, 1969), chapter 5

4. Their inconsistencies and shortcomings are discussed sympathetically in William O'Neill, *Coming Apart: An Informal History of America in the 1960s* (Chicago: Quadrangle Books, 1971), and in the books by Kenneth Keniston

5. For full details see John A. MacDonald, *House of Acts* (Carol Stream, Ill.: Creation House, 1970), pp. 49-86; Edward E. Plowman, *The Jesus Movement in America* (Elgin, Ill.: David C. Cook Publishing Co., 1971), pp. 44, 43, 37

6. See Pat King, *The Jesus People Are Coming* (Plainfield, N.J.: Logos International, 1971), pp. 3-29; and Ronald M. Enroth, Edward E. Ericson Jr., and C. Breckinridge Peters, *The Jesus People: Old-Time Religion in the*

Age of Aquarius (Grand Rapids: Wm. B. Eerdmans, 1972), pp. 13-15

7. See Enroth, et al., *The Jesus People,* pp. 104-05, for the full text. The most useful source of information on the CWLF is the reader edited by the Judson Press, *The Street People: Selections from "Right On!" Berkeley's Christian Underground Student Newspaper* (Valley Forge: Judson Press, 1971)

8. Enroth, et al., *The Jesus People,* pp. 102-114; *Street People,* pp. 10-11; Two Brothers from Berkeley, *Letters to Street Christians* (Grand Rapids: Zondervan, 1971)

9. Arthur Blessitt, *Turned On to Jesus* (New York: Hawthorn Books, 1971), pp. 143 ff. For the story of Blessitt's recent activities see Enroth, et al., *The Jesus People,* pp. 69-73

10. Roger C. Palms, *The Jesus Kids* (Valley Forge: Judson Press, 1971), pp. 42, 47. The Southern Baptist Convention *Home Missions* devoted its June/July, 1971 issue to the Jesus Movement; see pp. 13, 22 on drugs; Robert Lynn Adams and Robert John Fox, "Mainlining Jesus: The New Trip," *Society,* February, 1972, pp. 53-55; Blessitt, *Turned On to Jesus,* chs. 13-15; Brian Vachon, "The Jesus Movement Is Upon Us," *Look,* February 9, 1971, pp. 15-21.

11. Vachon, "The Jesus Movement," p. 20

12. Lowell D. Streiker, *The Jesus Trip: Advent of the Jesus Freaks* (Nashville: Abingdon Press, 1971), pp. 106-107; see also the discussion in Adams and Fox, "Mainlining Jesus"; Phil Tracy, "The Jesus Freaks: Savagery and Salvation on Sunset Strip," *Commonweal,* October 30, 1970, pp. 122-125

13. *Home Missions,* June/July, 1971, p. 16. This issue was reprinted as Walker L. Knight, compiler, *Jesus People Come Alive* (Wheaton: Tyndale House Publishers,

1971). See also Kenneth L. Woodward, "The Jesus People: Freak Out or Cop Out?", *Christian Herald,* September, 1971, pp. 12, 14

Chapter 5

1. See case studies in Streiker, *The Jesus Trip,* pp. 24-34, 79-89; *Home Missions,* June/July, 1971, pp. 53-63; and Enroth, et al., *Jesus People,* pp. 223-232

2. The most extensive critical studies to date are Enroth, et al, *Jesus People,* and Streiker, *The Jesus Trip*

3. Pederson, *Jesus People,* pp. 44 ff. This conclusion is supported in the other works on the movement by Palms, *The Jesus Kids,* Streiker, *The Jesus Trip,* and Plowman, *The Jesus Movement*

4. Pederson, *Jesus People,* p. 87

5. Streiker, *The Jesus Trip,* pp. 31, 38-39

6. pp. 20-23; the quotation, used with permission of Abingdon Press, is on pp. 21 and 23; Enroth, *et al, Jesus People,* pp. 58-59

7. Enroth, et al, *Jesus People,* pp. 137-143

8. "House of Miracles," *Lutheran Standard,* November 2, 1971, pp. 12-13

9. *Home Missions,* June/July, 1971, pp. 30-33

10. "The Man from Wayout," Wayout Publications, Hollywood, California. See also *Home Missions,* June/July, 1971, p. 57, and the series of pamphlets on Jesus published by the Christian World Liberation Front

11. An excellent example of this is the Christian World Liberation Front pamphlet, "God's Forever Family"

13. A more detailed discussion of this is in chapter 6

14. Enroth, et al, *The Jesus People,* pp. 194-206

15. Lindsay, *The Late Great Planet Earth* (Grand Rapids: Zondervan, 1970); *Home Missions,* June/July, 1971, pp. 56-67; Streiker, *The Jesus Trip,* pp. 69-78; Enroth, et al, *Jesus People,* pp. 179-193

16. "The New Rebel Cry: Jesus Is Coming!" *Time,* June 21, 1971, p. 59; Carl F. H. Henry, "Evangelical Pathbreaking," *Christianity Today,* May 8, 1970, p. 746; *The Street People: Selections from "Right On!",* p. 37; Palms, *The Jesus Kids,* p. 63

17. *Home Missions,* June/July, 1971, pp. 46, 36; a news item on Arthur Blessitt, *Christianity Today,* August 21, 1970, p. 1046; Rita Warren, "Fire for Jesus," *Decision,* February, 1971, p. 6; Palms, *The Jesus Kids,* pp. 67-68; Pederson, *Jesus People,* Adams and Fox, "Mainlining Jesus," *Society,* February, 1972, pp. 50-55

Chapter 6

1. See Robert N. Taylor, Jr., *This Damned Campus: As Seen by a College Chaplain* (Philadelphia: Pilgrim Press, 1969); and Albert H. Friedlander, ed., *Never Trust a God over 30: New Styles in Campus Ministry* (New York: McGraw-Hill, 1968), especially pp. 31-70

2. A news item in *Lutheran Standard,* November 2, 1971, p. 23

3. Robert E. Coleman, ed., *One Divine Moment* (Old Tappan, N.J.: Fleming H. Revell Co., 1970); news stories in *Christianity Today,* February 12, 1971, pp. 475-477

4. *Christianity Today,* May 22, 1970, p. 794

5. April 23, 1971, pp. 718, 720

6. Anon., "Preface," *Christ, The Liberator* (Downers Grove, Ill.: Inter-Varsity Press, 1971), p. 5

7. His speech is in *Christ, The Liberator,* pp. 189-191; © 1971 by Inter-Varsity Christian Fellowship. Used by permission from Inter-Varsity Press, Downers Grove, IL 60515; see also *Moody Monthly,* March, 1971, p. 75; *Christian Century,* February 17, 1971, pp. 226-227; *His,* March, 1971, pp. 5, 6; *Christianity Today,* January 29, 1971, pp. 425-426

8. David L. Warren, "A State of Quiet Calamity," *Commonweal,* March 3, 1972, p. 522; Richard Lovelace, "The Shape of the Coming Revival," *Christian Century,* October 6, 1971, pp. 1164-1167

9. See *Collegiate Challenge,* the Campus Crusade magazine, and two books by its director, Bill Bright: *Revolution Now* (1969) and *Come Help Change the World* (1971)

10. News story in *Christianity Today,* January 21, 1972, p. 378

11. News story in *Christianity Today,* March 3, 1972, p. 529

12. Lovelace, "The Shape of the Coming Revival," p. 1166

13. Linda Jacobson, "Passenger on the Bus," *Campus Fellowship* (Waco, Texas), Spring, 1971, p. 8

14. Plowman, *The Jesus Movement in America,* p. 111; Edward D. O'Connor, C.S.C., *The Pentecostal Movement in the Catholic Church* (Notre Dame, Ind.: Ava Maria Press, 1971), pp. 17-18; see also O'Connor's account in *Logos Journal,* September/October, 1971, p. 17

15. See the statement reprinted in O'Connor, *The Pentecostal Movement,* pp. 291-293

16. Kevin and Dorothy Ranaghan, eds., *As the Spirit Leads Us* (New York: Paulist Press, 1971), p. 13; copyright by Paulist Press and used by permission; J. Massingberd Ford, *The Pentecostal Experience* (New York: Paulist Press, 1970), *passim.*

17. Gelpi, *Pentecostalism: A Theological Viewpoint* (New York: Paulist Press, 1971), pp. 83-84; J. Massingberd Ford, *Baptism of the Spirit: Three Essays on the Pentecostal Experience* (Techny, Ill.: Divine Word Publications, 1971), ch. 1.

18. See the article on this subject by Edward Fiske in the *New York Times,* November 3, 1970, p. 56. See also Killian McDonnell, O.S.B., *Catholic Pentecostalism* (Pecos, New Mexico: Dove Publications, 1970). O'Connor, *The Pentecostal Experience,* has an extensive bibliography.

19. Michael I. Harrison, "The Organization of Commitment in the Catholic Pentecostal Movement," Ph.D. dissertation, Department of Sociology, University of Michigan, 1972

20. John C. Haughey, S.J., "The Jesus People of Ann Arbor," *America,* February 12, 1972, pp. 142-143

21. *Ibid.;* Janet Benedetti, "Pentecostalism in Ann Arbor, Looking for the Answer," *The Michigan Daily,* February 27, 1972, p. 4. These are, interestingly, also the "Four Spiritual Laws" distributed by Campus Crusade for Christ

22. *Ibid.*

23. *Ibid.;* Enroth, et al, *Jesus People,* pp. 202-206

Chapter 7

1. See an article by Bill Kovach in the *New York Times,* December 17, 1970, pp. 1, 84

2. See Dick Fairfield, *Communes, U.S.A.* (Baltimore: Penguin Books, 1972) on these groups, and the materials distributed on request by the Koinonia Partners, Americus, Ga. 31709; William Hedgepeth and Dennis Stock, *The*

Alternative (New York: The Macmillan Company, 1970)

3. See Michael Lerner, "Where To?", *Change,* September, 1971, pp. 26-33; Robert Houriet, *Getting Back Together* (New York: Coward, McCann and Geoghegan, Inc., 1971), *passim.* See also the several issues of the *Whole Earth Catalog,* and George R. Fitzgerald, *Communes: Their Goals, Hopes and Problems* (New York: Paulist Press, 1972)

4. Albin Wagner, "Drop City," *Avatar,* August 4, 1967, n.p.

5. Kovach, *New York Times,* December 17, 1970, p. 84. See also the information on these found in the titles listed in footnotes 2, 3, and 4 above

6. Houriet, *Getting Back Together,* p. 100. Copyright by Coward, McCann, and Geoghegan, and used by permission

7. *Ibid.*

8. *Ibid.,* pp. 101-102

9. Fairfield, *Communes, U.S.A.,* p. 186

10. Enroth, et al *Jesus People,* pp. 21-52

11. Pp. 26-27

12. *Ibid.;* Plowman, *The Jesus Movement,* pp. 60-61. Streiker, *The Jesus Trip,* p. 53; an article by Plowman in *Christianity Today,* November 5, 1971, p. 147

13. Enroth, et al, *Jesus People,* pp. 34, 208-211

14. See the letter to the editor by a parent in *Time,* February 14, 1972, p. 4

15. Reprinted in Plowman, *The Jesus Movement,* pp. 59-60

16. Enroth, et al, *Jesus People,* p. 40

17. Pp. 48-53 news items in *Christianity Today,* November

5, 1971, pp. 146, 148; December 17, 1971, p. 291; *Newsweek,* November 22, 1971, p. 90; and an article on the Children of God in the Green Sheet, *Milwaukee Journal,* October 18, 1971, pp. 1, 2

18. "Fellow Traveling with Jesus," *Time,* September 6, 1971, p. 54; Enroth, et al, *Jesus People,* pp. 13-14, 152

19. Two of the most important of the many studies by Wierwille are: *The Bible Tells Me So* and *The New Dynamic Church*

20. See The Way brochure on "Power for Abundant Living," n.d., and another "What Is the Way?"

21. Enroth, et al, *Jesus People,* pp. 152, 198

22. *Ibid. Time,* September 6, 1971, p. 54 see also "The Bookstore Catalog, 1971"

23. Peter Rowley, *New Gods in America* (New York: David McKay Company, 1971), p. 141, and also pp. 137-143

24. P. ix

25. Pp. 163-74. The quotation is on p. 170

For Further Reading

Enroth, Ronald M., Edward E. Ericson, Jr., and C. Breckinridge Peters. *The Jesus People: Old-Time Religion in the
Age of Aquarius.* Grand Rapids: William B. Eerdmans Co.,
1972.

The most thorough study of the teen-age groups now in
print. It assumes considerable theological knowledge by
the reader.

Fairfield, Dick. *Communes, USA.* San Francisco: Alternatives
Foundation, 1971. Published in 1972 by Penguin Books
under the same title.

This has brief but very helpful information on the whole
spectrum of communes. It also has the best bibliography
and mailing addresses on this subject in print.

Ford, Clay. *Berkeley Journal: Jesus and the Street People—A Firsthand Report.* New York: Harper and Row, 1972.

A fascinating summer diary of a seminary student who worked among street people around Berkeley. Good analysis and some objective criticism make this a valuable primary source of information on the teen-age groups in the movement.

Graham, Billy. *The Jesus Generation.* Grand Rapids: Zondervan, 1971.

Sermons to the Jesus kids rather than about them. Heavy on personal anecdotal references, short on analysis

Kildahl, Dr. John T. *The Psychology of Speaking in Tongues.* New York: Harper and Row, 1972.

The most thoroughly documented study of this movement from a scholar trained in both theology and clinical psychology.

Knight, Walter L., compiler. *Jesus People Come Alive.* Wheaton: Tyndale House, 1971.

A brief, impressionistic interpretation, very sympathetic.

Moody, Jess. *The Jesus Freaks.* Waco, Texas: Word, 1971.

Very helpful in that it presents extensive writings—poetry, essays, reflections—by several Jesus people whom he interviewed. It also has The Berkeley Free Church Directory.

Ortega, Ruben, compiler. *The Jesus People Speak Out!* New York: Pyramid Books, 1972.

A compilation of brief statements to interviewers on a wide variety of issues—theology, parents, sex, war, drugs.

Palms, Roger C., *The Jesus Kids.* Valley Forge: Judson Press, 1971.

A good summary of the major themes in the teen-age phase.

Plowman, Edward E. *The Jesus Movement in America.* Elgin, Ill.: David C. Cook Publishing Co., 1971.

An excellent journalistic account by one of the important figures in the early part of the movement. One only wishes it was longer.

Ranaghan, Kevin and Dorothy, eds., *As The Spirit Leads Us.* New York: Paulist Press, 1971.

A collection of essays by leading proponents of Pentecostalism within the Roman Catholic Church. All favor the movement.

Streiker, Lowell D. *The Jesus Trip: Advent of the Jesus Freaks.* Nashville: Abingdon, 1971.

The most critical of the shorter studies. Based on brief personal observations and personal judgments.

Williams, Donald M. *Call to the Streets.* Minneapolis: Augsburg, 1972.

By the youth minister of Hollywood Presbyterian Church. It has several illuminating biographical accounts of how an establishment church works closely with street people.

Acknowledgements

I wish to thank St. Olaf College for a generous grant covering the professional typing of this manuscript. Special thanks to Steve Miles and Harold Otterlei of St. Olaf, and Dr. Ronald Teigen of the University of Michigan. My best friend and closest reader is my wife Helen.